I write this to encourage the brave to be braver…it is going to take courage to make the trip of a life time. There is something I need to tell so that you can understand the reason and will of the mind of a man trying to tell the story of his life with an expectancy of five years from the time of a diagnosis.

I am that, Chicken Scratch, can you read it?

Life has been a struggle for me from birth and looks like all the way to the grave, yet I am holding on to something. What is it? Why the will? Read the scratch if you can…

*John Robinson*

# CHICKEN SCRATCH

An Autobiography
By JOHN ROBINSON

**iSeebookz Publishing LLC**
**Lagrange Georgia**

*Chicken Scratch*
Copyright © 2018 by John Robinson All rights reserved.

*Printed in the United States of America. No part of this publication may be used or reproduced, stored in a retrieval system, transmitted in any form or by any means- electronic, mechanical, photocopy, recording, or by any information storage and retrieval system, except for brief quotations in printed reviews, without the prior written permission of the publisher.*

iSeebookz Publishing LLC
137B Commerce Ave Suite 300
LaGrange GA 30241

Book Design Copyright © 2018 by Robinson

Book illustrations by John Robinson
Cover design by Sheldon Rolins and Cheryl Litton
Interior design by Priscilla Sodeke
*Editor: Nicole Dixon

ISBN: 978-0-9995869-2-1

Biography/Autobiography/Personal Memoirs
*Minimal editing to maintain authentic integrity*

*Although the author and publisher have made every effort to ensure that the information in this book was correct at press time, the author and publisher do not assume and hereby disclaim any liability to any party for any loss, damage, or disruption caused by errors or omissions, whether such errors or omissions result from negligence, accident, or any other cause.*

First Edition: 2018

10 9 8 7 6 5 4 3 2 1

## Solid

A stone, we know is solid, not like water, it's just a stone
See, water is something all living things need;
I mean all things of life that lives.

But the stone is just a stone
Until you shape it into a sculpture or a building block

To build solid character, like the stone
Shaping the personality into something solid
It is transformed by time to its natural form or
Common shape that nature itself builds
Displaying a state of the art and beauty,
Formed by its natural behavior taking on single grains

Our lives are much like the stone,
Accumulating scars of time as we age, one day at the time
Month by month, year by year until we reach the peak of life's mountain,
Then have a stone placed over our heads that replicates a real stone of time.

We are that too; think, see, feel, touch, hear, and smell

The poor soul of man, the stone of all ages, just think,
You and I are one of these stones.

The pillars of society rest upon that stone called Jesus the Chief Cornerstone.
We need the Lord more than we need water, because Jesus is life itself.

When the world throws stones at you, "It's just a stone against a stone,"
Remember they both are solid, the weaker one will shatter and only
The strong survive and qualify to be a cornerstone, and that's solid.

—John Robinson

# CONTENTS

DEDICATION . . . . . . . . . . . . . . . . . . . . . . . . . . . . . . . . .iv

FOREWORD . . . . . . . . . . . . . . . . . . . . . . . . . . . . . . . . .vi

PROLOGUE . . . . . . . . . . . . . . . . . . . . . . . . . . . . . . . . . .x

CHAPTER ONE . . . . . . . . . . . . . . . . . . . . . . . . . . . . . . . 1

CHAPTER TWO . . . . . . . . . . . . . . . . . . . . . . . . . . . . . . 18

CHAPTER THREE . . . . . . . . . . . . . . . . . . . . . . . . . . . . . 34

CHAPTER FOUR . . . . . . . . . . . . . . . . . . . . . . . . . . . . . . 43

CHAPTER FIVE . . . . . . . . . . . . . . . . . . . . . . . . . . . . . . . 70

CHAPTER SIX . . . . . . . . . . . . . . . . . . . . . . . . . . . . . . . . 87

CHAPTER SEVEN . . . . . . . . . . . . . . . . . . . . . . . . . . . . . 98

# DEDICATION

**I WOULD LIKE TO DEDICATE** this book to my wife Terrie Lynette Robinson who was and still is my hero. We have been married for 40 plus years. She is a wife, mother and a friend. Terrie held the family together through the 12 unbearable stormy years. She is the shoulder of comfort during the hours of distress; no greater love other than that of God could have been shown. She was there for us.

# FOREWORD

## BY JACK SCAROLA AND MARVIN DUNN

### Jack Scarola

**WHEN I FIRST MET JOHN** Robinson there was nothing about his physical appearance to inform me that I was meeting a giant of a man. There was no way to measure the long and crooked path he had wandered, how many detours and dead ends he had encountered along that path, or the pain he had to endure during his journey.

What I did soon learn in my role as one of John's lawyers—and all that really mattered at the time—was that John was a natural leader with the strength and courage to stand up to oppression. I also learned much later, as John's legal battle dragged on for years, that against all odds, John had the remarkable perseverance to see his battle to a successful conclusion.

The readers of *Chicken Scratch* are about to embark on a poetic journey into the heart and mind of a Black American hero, but nothing at the start of that journey points to the triumph at the end. John takes us through his early, loveless childhood, raised in poverty, the victim of abuse by one parent and neglect by the other. Indeed, John's early life is anything but promising and includes a 5 year jail sentence at age 14.

Readers will stand alongside John Robinson as he confronts the late Twentieth Century remnants of a mentality that is still capable of imposing the shackles of Deep South racial bigotry on an entire workforce. And then they will accompany John on the life-and-death struggle in which he is now engaged. Prepare to hear the unique voice of John Robinson, but there is nothing that can truly prepare anyone for "chicken scratch"

*Jack Scarola an honors graduate from Georgetown University is a Personal Injury Attorney in Florida.*

## Dr. Marvin Dunn

John Robinson is one of the bravest men ever to have walked in Florida. This is no overstatement. John Robinson, my friend, has penned a compelling story of survival in a racist South. I can personally attest to much of what is written here because I have known the man and his family for over thirty years. I bore witness to his travails in his federal lawsuit against one of the most powerful men in America. I saw his children grow up under the most oppressive conditions. I was pleased and proud to have been retained by his attorneys to provide psychological testimony as to the impact of racial oppression on John and the other members of the class that joined his historic suit. I witnessed his decline into cancer and his ascendency out of it.

Few black men would have done or did do what Robinson did although millions felt the same bite of discrimination. Robinson had to survive his own father who abused and disrespected him. He had to raise himself out of a life of crime and ultimately by his own tenacity of faith, be delivered up to God as clearly he has been. The John Robinson story requires guts to read. He is raw in describing his physical pain and that of his wife but he is no less definitive in describing the pain of delinquency, race discrimination and poverty. John Robinson is a genius. The things that he learned and did in the course of his life could only have been absorbed and put into practice by the mind of a genius. This is a riveting account of how that Robinson genius and guts played out during a very dark era of American history.

*Dr. Marvin Dunn, historian, organizer and a retired professor emeritus from Florida International University.*

# PROLOGUE

**MY NAME IS JOHN HENRY** Robinson and I am a sixty year old man. I am writing this to encourage the brave to be even braver.

On March 10, 2008, I was diagnosed with Esophageal Cancer, which was malignant and terminal. I was given two to six months at most to live, but the Lord saw fit that I live longer. I had a large tumor above my stomach with a tree stem like system with roots down through the esophagus and into my stomach. The doctor found a nesting of small tumors on my left side and a colony of tumors on my right side. I underwent several tests because the cancer I had was very aggressive. Dr. Farquhar, who found the cancer referred me to a surgeon named Dr. W. Harvey Miller. Dr. Miller stated he wanted to do an examination before he did anything, surgery included; because looking at the medical report he saw very little hope for me. His examination would allow him to decide if he needed to remove the tumor or if I should get radiation and chemotherapy. So he scheduled an endoscopy. About a week after my examination Dr. Miller called my wife and I to his office and informed us of his thoughts based upon his findings. His exact words were; "My friend you might have a chance; at first there wasn't much at all. Dr. Farquhar found a nesting of tumors on your left side and a colony on your right side. I only found the large tumor and two scars where the other tumors were. I don't know what happened to them, or where they went. I only saw scars. This means that you were in the fourth stage and somehow, something set you back to the third stage." He then explained to me that my lymph nodes were positive; and that was how the cancer spread to the rest of my body. The cancer cell he described was a life cell, a smart cell. This cancer cell mutates, adapts, fights to live and outsmarts the medical world; it manages to hide itself most of the time.

The only cure is to try and remove it surgically. You pray that you get it all and it doesn't resurface because it is a life cell just one more than the body requires, thus the deadly cancer is reactivated. He informed us that it was going to be a rough road ahead with surgery and after the radiation and chemotherapy treatments. He drew a diagram of my esophagus, heart, stomach and pancreas inside a block area and said; "The only hope for you, is to remove everything in the block area. Your heart will be moved, the esophagus tube behind your heart will be cut, your stomach and your pancreas and those most positive lymph nodes around your stomach area will also be removed. It's going to be a rough ride, but I'm one of the best in my field, I have special training beyond the common doctor." I thought to myself; "What choices do I have? My plane just crashed and I survived the fall. I reckon I'd better just pick up the pieces that remain" (Chicken scratch)... Can you read it? Do you understand it? It's life.

Before I go any farther let me tell you something that I believe set me back from the fourth stage of cancer to the third stage. Because Dr. Miller told me that I would be taking radiation treatment as part of my cancer therapy, I got up one morning, took a large four inch diameter magnifying glass, and on my grandchildren trampoline I would lay down on my back. I'd remove my shirt and let the sun light shine through the glass on the area they told me the tumors were located. I held that glass just far enough from my skin to not burn me, but when it felt like it was about to burn I would remove it. I repeated this several times and consistently around eleven o'clock am. I did this for at least five days in a row, then every other day until I saw Dr. Harvey Miller. In my most humble opinion I believe the rays from the sun killed those younger tumor cells, the larger one was advanced beyond treatment of any kind, it had to be removed. Even with surgery my life expectancy was only five years. I'm 60 years old and that was six years ago and I'm still in remission.

June 11, 2008 the surgery took place it was another step through hell's gate. I was there before. I fought the cancer of racism in the United States Federal Court in Miami Florida Case # 83-8655 Civil- Hoeveler on the scale of Justice tried by the weights of laws, balanced by the interpretation of attorneys. Mr. Moses Baker, John Scarola, Jeffrey Peterson, Peter Helwig, Debbie Singer, and others were the team. The now Honorable Federal Judge Moses Baker was my Moses in the wilderness sent by God to fight my battle. John Scarola known as Jack Scarola the owner of the Island Of Malta was my power pack among the giants of law. He and Mr. Baker as they say in the hood "Walked the Dog" in the courtroom. They were superb. Jeffrey Peterson was the one that took my case and filed it in the United States Federal Court. Peter Helwig was at the time the head attorney for Florida Rural Legal Services for clients that could not afford an attorney. Now, Mr. Helwig is in private practice fighting discrimination. Debbie Singer the fireball of them all; was the paralegal, the investigator that would not leave any stone unturned. I also had the famous David Lipman on my team the attorney that won the cases for civil rights for Black folks throughout the south. I had Willie Gary, of Stuart Florida on my team at first with the Equal Employment Opportunity Commission charge, which got me the Notice of Right to Sue. His brother was my neighbor for twenty three years, I knew Mr. Gary as Edward Gary, a friend. I had a team that fought to the end, not only for me but for many Blacks and Whites that were discriminated while employed at Caulkins. The very Caulkins who was the husband of Eleanor Newman-Caulkins the First lady of Opera in Denver Colorado. Those old tongue worn words, I can't read that chicken scratch; it was the pride of the proud, the vision of progression of the oppressed. "It is the undefined that causes the eye not to identify a scratch or impression, that personal private perimeter; built from pride, dignity, and gut. (Chicken Scratch)

## What does it all mean?

The words "chicken scratch" is a form of slang honed out of the past and is still today just as common as it was then. It was used to define the appearance of a person's handwriting when it is difficult to read. However, behind these words is a special history willed by time, as a part of the black American struggle, twisting, spell bending, sometimes breaking the will of those trying to define the symbols of the struggle; integrated segregation. (CHICKEN SCRATCH) CAN YOU READ IT?

Behind these words is a special history willed by time. The breaking down of a culture expressed through hardships. As you can see from above, I used the word spell bending not spellbinding (chicken scratch) DO you see it? It was used to express a hidden meaning of an expression to define the need of an education to reach a higher standard in life. Discrimination, bending our will toward breaking, never letting up, relentlessly pressing the will of our spirit, in the quest of capturing the mind, but the spell bending effect is the mirror effect of the oppressor's heart from his hateful unyielding will. The rebellious mind of my descendants, refused to be enslaved mentally, physically, or spiritually. Singing the song of rebellion, I want to be free by faith and education, we may one day in time reach a higher state of being. The majority of people will not talk about the real issues of today, the black world. (Chicken Scratch) Did you read it?

What is it to be black or what it is about being black in America? A nation plagued by deception, like from rags to riches, the mix down of a race of a people. Do we truly understand the weather forecast for such a storm? If so, it would just blow you away. (Chicken Scratch) Read that.

The storm of life always seems to just keep on raging. The dreamers of freedom raise these issues about the race, moving ahead not the race card. It's the fact of knowing that you are not who you may have been if history would have told another story about our past of from whence we came, the west coast African slave. The problems we have, is that people live to tell the story. Therefore, it is possible for us not to know everything about where we came from. Even though many were stripped of their dignity, some of them held on to what they had, and would never let it go, because it is something built from within. (Chicken Scratch) Could you read it?

It's the unchanging experience matched throughout modern day time. We must hold on and be willing to die just to keep it. When we were diagnosed of being free, medicated by the whip, broke from the will to learn, deprived of all joy, and the will of being family, we became the black American slave. Yet we felt something inside saying hold on black man, daylight is coming in a little while. We may be in the dark, in a blind nation but there is a light shining farther than the eye can see, just hold on. How great is the stand and we have already withstood the brunt of the storm; educate our children to pray to the ever seeing GOD, scale the highest mountain and then reach for the stars (Chicken Scratch).

We must soar in our flight, taking off with positive traction and expect nothing less than a positive reaction. Believe it or not, it is in people to excel. It has nothing to do with color, race, religion or origin; it's just in all humanity. Speaking as a minister, we must pray that we can all overcome together as a people on a global scale, but first we need to work on home right here in America. It seems like every local government is setting an example for its neighbor on how to practice exclusion, something that title six prohibits. A method of systematic injustice, rules and regulations designed as status, with amendments appearing to be legal by common sight and law. Too complex to balance in the court of law with lengthy trails in some cases. Designed to lean in favor of the rules and it is sad to say, below all of the cosmetics the rule is to discriminate with extreme prejudice. Although we have a black president he is blinded by a republican congress. History will show and tell the full story of him being the first black man as President of the United States of America. The hell he would catch behind the scenes, the most talked about and hated President other than Lincoln. With the nation split, he had to give away large sums of money, allow criminals to rape and rob the treasury to the point where it caused the world markets to tip and a lot of them failed, like major world banks; because he made history it shook the world. John Boehner speaker of the house lead the republicans nearly to doom, he set this nation on the cliff and caused a major shutdown, the question is what history will show about him. (CHICKEN SCRATCH) politic that!

When we scan our minds for reasons; how could we not think of the race factor? Speaking about race, this high profile mythology of discrimination is set and fixed as part of the American fabric to keep and maintain the power. Even though Crispus Attucks lead the way and was the first to die in the revolutionary war a Black man or an American, it didn't help us; the poor is still poor, the homeless are still homeless, sleeping under our bridges and trees. The industry of ghetto economic, governmental food stamp assistance is a fraud program, a form of institutionalized slavery to the American taxpayer, is operating at full steam ahead no change just charge. Now is our time, do we see the progress we have made, all we need to do now is to redirect our finances, by purchasing from our own stores, something we should have been doing ever since we were freed. Invest with banks, stores, accountant offices, medical offices, retail stores and anyone, we do business with, that will return the monies and benefits back into the community or neighborhood.

Self-empowerment and education is a portion of the key factors that will lead to change. It is time to load up and throw our ministers out of our communities that still continue to preach that same old economic enslavement past down from generation to generation. They are not teaching the factors of life as Jesus did. They are preaching for big bill. That's the most harmful thing to the black community because they are not concerned over the death of its economy. Not realizing the danger of not teaching the power of economics and to serve in one's lifetime as a contributor, a function that everyone is a part of. We must contribute something of value to be a real asset from your own personal values. Realize that you are your greatest asset, because greater is the gifts that is within you than the fancies that is of this world.

# CHAPTER ONE

**AS I AM SITTING HERE** looking back over my life. There once was a time when, I would not have glanced back, to possibly see if there was anything I would change. This old life has truly been a road of travel; I am a 60 year old man. I was born April 21st 1954 in the back woods on a farm off of Stafford Wright Road in Cherry Creek by a midwife. My grandfather's place was approximately 250 acres or more of good prime farmland; of course, there was no market for his product. We were in Lowndes County, Valdosta, Georgia.

But, we lived from the land. We sold some of our products through whites and to each other. As I look back I am amazed at what a person could withstand. Just think, living

in a racist nation without any rights, freed just a few years with nothing in your pockets nor in your head, and over a few years we learn to read some, but with little comprehension. (Chicken Scratch) did you comprehend that?

Anyway, on that old farm, I felt so good I was indeed free, the air was a better quality, the birds' songs sounded better, the sky was a little bit bluer and time was better. Now I need to know, where, did it all go? I fear those days are forever gone. I loved my grandfather, I cherished the ground he walked on, and he was a very good person. I never heard a profane word out of his mouth, he treated my grandmother like she was his true queen; they were farmers. I lived with them for three years, from the ages of six to nine; I truly enjoyed those three years. Allow me to explain the reason I lived with my grandparents. My father died in 1960 at the age of 32 from cancer. His name was Ralph Shiver, he was born in 1928. My mother, Louise Shanks, was born 1929 and she lived to be 81, she died in May of 2011. My mom was 25 years old when she gave birth to me. She and dad didn't "tie the knot" as they say. Mom met a gentleman by the name of Rufus Robinson in 1958 and they got married. I was his child until my sister was born in 1960, the very year my father died. When my mother nursed my sister, she was not allowed to put my sister out of her hands to do anything for me, his love turned to hate towards me. He would beat and kick mama around if she put my sister down to see about me, and I was only 6 years old. So I spent more time at my grandma's house than I spent at home.

Rufus treated me with hate behind my mother's back. He had this Ford Crown Victoria, two tone red and white that would out run grease lighting, they say. (Chicken Scratch) did you hear it! Well one time when I was seven I spent the weekend at home. I had no idea this was the weekend of weekends for me. Early Saturday morning Rufus went outside to crank his car and it would not start, he had left the lights on and the battery was dead. So he went and got a ford tractor from his boss for me to pull the car and crank it. The only problem with that was I had never been on a tractor. I never had my hands on a gear shifter or anything like that before in my little life. So he hooks the chain from the tractor to the automobile then pulls the throttle on the tractor around 2500 rpms, puts my foot on the clutch and tells me to hold it down until he say let it go. Thank God he got the gear mixed up and put it in reverse, if not I would have been gone. I had a hard time holding that clutch down. When he said let it go; boy did I. The tractor jumped backwards, punched a big hole in the radiator and bent the front of the car really bad. With the wheel bent against the car, and the tractor shut down, Rufus jumped out the car; but not to see if I was okay. He clenched his fist and punched me in the face as hard as he could; which knocked me off to the other side of the tractor. Blood like liver came from my mouth and nose until it clogged. (Chicken Scratch) Can you read IT?

That man showed me what hate really was. I knew the love I had from my mom and her parents. This man Rufus Robinson, whom I bear the name, hated me. Another time his father came over and sat on our front porch, he called out to my mother, he said "Whore get me a glass of water." My mom froze in her tracks, she asked, "What did you say!" he said, "Whore gets me a glass of water that's what I said." Mom said "I am not getting you nothing;" he said "Son kick her ass and I mean kick it good. I hate all of those damn Shanks." Rufus beat my mom, he sat down on top of her and he continued to beat her. I found a coca cola bottle and hit him in the back of the head. He jumped up off my mom and chased after me, I ran. It was good it was dark, from fear I jumped over into a deep well I held on to the side, God held me up from falling to my death. The only thing that kept me here was my big toe and nail. My left foot found an opening in the stone that made the well. The toenail broke half way down the toe, and the pain was very bad. I was scared fearless. When I heard the car leave, I didn't know if my mom was dead or alive, I pulled myself out of the well and fell upon the ground. I heard someone; I jumped and ran into a tree and hid, and would not come out. Then I heard the voice I loved, my mom. When I came out she was naked, I went into the house and got a white sheet and put over her, and lead her through the woods to grandma and granddad's house. Yes of course I hated my sister's father, a man called Rufus Robinson. Well, we all left Georgia with him, soon after that he and mom separated. Later, mom met a boxer named Elijah Wiggins; her life was still bad but it was somewhat better than it was before; they stayed together for 40 years until Eli died. I was 10 years old when they met. Due to the life of hell Rufus put me through; I gave Elijah a hard time. I turned to the streets. I saw the real deal, the bottom rail of the true underworld. (Chicken Scratch) Could you read that?

Elijah Wiggins was born and raised in Baton Rouge, Louisiana on the South side; this is the City of Harm. A place of the real ghetto life but pride, street stalked of warriors. You either kick ass or get your ass kicked simple as that. You

## CHICKEN SCRATCH

had to stand to understand the hood, the weak could not survive the streets, unless you were straight cut to be somebody the pride of the hood, a person of a special quality, or some form of disability, other than that you had to roll. (Chicken Scratch) Can you see it? Elijah was a felon; he did 6 years in the big house state prison for attempted murder. He went three times and did 2 years each time or more. He was a very good man that just didn't play at all. He picked fruit as a migrant worker even though he had the skills as a brick mason, auto mechanic, and a barber. He was very good at these trades. But when you questioned him about why he picked, he would say, "I like to be my own boss, besides you earn your money." He and I had a real rocky relationship, I could not be fair with him because of the way Rufus had treated me (Chicken Scratch). On the other hand mom caught hell, Eli was his nickname, he would beat her very badly, causing her face to be twisted up and her eyes were black, he would beat her down, and I couldn't take it. I was 12 years old and watched this type of shit over and over. I had to go. So one day we were picking apples in a field located 12 miles from Benton Harbor Michigan, in fact we lived out in the country, on Mr. Handy's farm. Anyway, that day Eli felt we weren't working hard enough, we were like a family of slaves. He said, "If you can't do no better than that go home;" so I took my sister and we went home. Once I got to the house I packed my rags into a brown paper bag, told my sister Dorothy, "One day I will be back for you, I love you, and tell mom it will be okay." I ran away, found an old empty single room box house in the middle of a field with no lights or water. (Chicken Scratch) Can you read it?

## CHICKEN SCRATCH

I could see the stars through the roof at night, and I got wet from the rain, I would pick berries through the day for a guy, sometimes mom and Eli would drive by and act like they didn't see me. When I was hungry and needed to take a bath, the guy I picked the berries for would pay me and let me bathe in an outside shower he had at his shop from a tank elevated in the air and heated from the natural sunlight. What I didn't know was that he knew Eli, and that Eli trimmed his grapes every year, so they were teaching me a lesson they knew I would never forget in life. I would walk to the store about a half mile from the shack in the field. Once at the store I would buy what I could, steal the rest or take a bite out of what I wanted. I was unaware that the store owner saw me each time and he acted as if he didn't see me. Again I didn't know Eli and mom traded with him and they were paying him for the things I stole or damaged. Then he gave me hell and called the law, at the same time he got me, I just knew that was it. But when the law came it was not for me, he didn't mention anything about me. I was standing there sweating hard, hoping I wasn't going to jail, I didn't know what to do or think. Well, he let me go and I went back to the field to that old lonely shack. Sitting on the side of a board I had for a bed I heard a car pull up, it was Eli. He sounded the horn; I went out. He said "Get in man," and he shut the car off. He said; "That woman won't let me sleep. I can't rest she keeps me up all night long, saying Eli you think he's alright? Will you go? Well, here I am." Eli continued, "Look man, I know I am not your daddy but Lou is all you got in this world. If you hurt anybody in this world don't ever let it be Lou. Don't worry about me—hell I might do anything, but Lou is all you got. Don't hurt Lou. Get your stuff and let's go home. I paid the man at the store. I had the man to let you pick berries. Don't you ever steal like you did at the store; I asked them to call the police." In my heart I felt that... (Chicken Scratch)... What about that?

In the area there were other migrant camps; on these camps you could find every type of persons in life; from men of God, to stone cold killers, wine heads, junkies, dancers, and singers. They had joints in the woods on these camps. The harvesting contractors set gambling houses on the camps; they would roll from Friday evening until Monday morning. Eli had me to keep the car from getting blocked, and to be ready at any given moment to dip or leave in a hurry. Eli taught me how to drive in our 1957 big block hemi. I remember on two occasions we had to leave in the heat of the moment. He would jump in the car and say "Drive!" I could drive, I would have dust up the road and everything along the way until Eli, would tell me to stop and get in the back seat.

He would get to the house at 2am and tell mom to pack up, and say, "Let's go to Baton Rouge or Florida." I knew we had the money from the gambling house, we rolled to the south side of Baton Rouge, Louisiana to harm city. We stayed there during the summer and then go back to Michigan when the season was over. By this time I was 13. I met four new friends; two sets of brothers named Lonnie and Charles Day along with Fred and Eddie Amos. Fred died about 4 months after we met from Rheumatic Fever, it was sad to see him with his hands, face, and feet swollen from the illness.

Eddie became like a brother to me, the brother I didn't have, we were true friends. Eddie had asthma really bad. We had one thing in common both our fathers were dead.

One Friday night Eli and mom had a few words and it led to him beating on mom. I walked away from the house and lay down on a trailer Mr. Handy used to load apples. There I gazed into the great beyond, the midnight blue sky and the stars. I asked God to give me a new life with 4 sons and a good wife, but from that point on I did not give a damn. I got off the trailer and walked several miles to Eddie Amos' house. We decided to take whatever we wanted and we did just that. From that night on I have never been the same, all the bullshit was over for man and beast in my book. (Chicken Scratch) Do you see?

At the age of 13 we promised not to be disrespectful to our elders stay perfect in their eyes, but hell on the rest, we robbed. Our thing was breaking and entering. Mom and Eli looked for me but couldn't find me. Eli would talk to me, after I'd try to ease into the house. I'd tell him, "Yes sir," and the very next day I'd go to jail for robbery. He and mom spent what little money they had trying to get me out of jail and on the right track. But I would get out, act right for a day or two, and then get back into my crime mode. I robbed my teachers, beat down the bully of the school, leave him for dead, and at the same time be the nice guy. From that point on I could not attend any schools in the county. Eli drove me 30 miles to a school in Indiana; but that didn't last (Chicken Scratch) what happened?

Mr. Handy being a rich white man got me back in school in the county. I started to act right for a little while until a blizzard came and the bus driver put my sister out on the road alone to walk in the storm. When she got home she had ice on one side of her face. The next day when I got on the bus, I asked the driver, Mr. Wheeler, why did he put my sister off the bus to walk home in the storm. He told me that the snow had covered the road and he could not bring her home, and that he put her off the bus. That was when I hit him with a mini baseball bat on the head he fell off the seat onto the floor. Now I'm expelled from school. Mr. Handy had to help me again to get into school. He complained on the driver for putting my sister's life in danger. The only thing was I couldn't ride the bus. One morning on my way to school Eli asked me to drop some clothes off to the dry cleaners and gave me $60.00 to pay for the clothes to be cleaned. I dropped the clothes off at the cleaners.

I spotted my friend Eddie he asked me what I was doing and I told him. I asked him if he felt like robbing the "Chicken Coop" a place like Kentucky Fried Chicken; he said it's up to me, then I said, "Let's see." So we went to the "Chicken Coop," and we put on the charm. The nice lady that worked there said, "You two young men seem so polite what can I get you?" We robbed her, dumped a drum of flour over her head and made her sit down in the corner until we left. Eddie had an asthma attack; he can't run and I can't leave him, I took him behind a J.C. Penny's which was a new construction project. We sat down in a trench that was dug for a water line, a German shepherd rushed upon us and that was it. My new life that I asked God to give... it took off. (Chicken Scratch)

That night, we went to jail for armed robbery and 7 other counts that we fit the description for. We stayed in jail for 90 days without bond before the trial. We got five years each at the age of 14. We were in Hungry Joe. The jail where you get one cup of coffee that tasted like it was made from cigar butts, a donut as hard as a baseball for breakfast; lunch was one slice of bread with one slice of cheese—that's it, and there was no dinner. This place, if a man comes in weighing 285 lbs, the medics take him out at 85lbs. Hungry Joe earned its name. It had no windows only florescent lighting; you could get your days and nights mixed up in there. The reason I know, is because I got my days mixed up. Mom came to visit me at 3:00 p.m. and I thought it was 3:00 a.m. because of the light system. When mom visited, we only saw each other's eyes through a small window with a speaker below it. Some of the types of ill treatment at the jail; we stayed in our 10'x10' cells the entire time, the door never opened. Eddie and I were in the same cell, and Eddie had an asthma attack, a real bad one that caused him to pass out. I yelled out for help, every cell yelled out. The guard finally came, and when he opened the cell he saw Eddie on the floor. He told me to get back, so I stepped back. The guard put one foot on each side of Eddie. He reached down grabbed Eddie by the collar with his left hand and reached toward heaven with his right hand then pulled rage down to Eddie's face. He slapped Eddie backward and forward yelling get up, get up! I began to yell at the guard to stop and then I jumped on his back. We went a couple of rounds until the other guards took me down. They took Eddie to the hospital and from there he escaped. I knew where he was. His mother came and begged me to tell her. I told her so they would not kill him. They did a few years later and got away with murder. This was my friend, and as I sit here some forty years later it seems like yesterday. (Chicken Scratch)

Well, Eddie got brought back to the jail and was put back into our cell. We were on the floor with the older men not with the minors. They tried to talk trash to scare us but they found out that we were nothing like them; we were that other generation, the one that did not give a damn about Mr. Charlie nor his crew. Believe it or not they respected us and started telling us we did not need that kind of a life; they were just fucked up and we were well on our way headed down the same path. Then one day a man came to the jail recruiting young men whose lives had been victimized by the system.

The dawn of days this was in 1967 Martin Luther King Jr. was still our hero the nation was in a reformation period and it was sweeping the land. Artists like James Brown singing songs like "Say It Loud I'm Black and I'm Proud," groups like the Impressions singing songs like if you had a *Choice of Color*; this was the spirit of the times. The nation was split by racism for the struggles of an emerging people. Eddie and I got trapped by the laws of the new system, and became victims of the feeble minds of oppressed men. In every transition of the times there were those that fought by the spirit of time for equilibrium, balance of justice and equality. One of these was the hero of my life, a man named Mr. David Mullins. He was that man that stopped by Hungry Joe jail recruiting the misfits of society, Eddie Amos and John Robinson.

# CHAPTER TWO

**EDDIE AND I WERE FACING** five years; two years on the potato farms on the outside of Chicago Heights and the rest of the time was to be spent in the State Penitentiary. Mr. David Mullins was the founder of a new experimental school called the Pioneer School, for boys like Eddie and I. He had the court to reconsider our position for rehabilitation at his school. It was not easy but he did get it done; he got us there. This was the point for the new beginning; the ending of stage one in my life. (Chicken Scratch) What on earth was God getting me ready for?

The day came when he met with Eddie and me one on one. He met with Eddie first. When he and I met he was very clean. I knew this man was somebody and that he had power to be in this position, as a black man. Mr. Mullins asked for my reasons, how I ended up in a place like Hungry Joes, a place where a young man like me had no reason to be. He told me he could get me out. I asked him, "How?" If I was facing five years, how was he going to get me out? He said he had a school called The Pioneer School for young brothers like me. (Chicken Scratch) Mullins?

Mr. Mullins had room for two more students; he asked if I was willing to change my life. I was ready. He requested information as to what type of work my parents did and if we were migrant workers. I told him we picked fruit and we were migrant workers. However, Mr. Mullins already knew the type of work we did. He had his reasons for questioning me. He wanted to know how I felt about doing that kind of work, moving from place to place, never calling a location home. I hated it. It wasn't the life I wanted; it wasn't a life, but it was a living.

At first it was great because I saw different places and met new people, but it got real. This was a way of life, and I got trapped in the zone of it, a place I did not care to be. (Chicken Scratch)

Yes, I would give this up if he could help me. I told him, I was willing to try. "Ok," he said and then questioned me about my friend Eddie. Mullins was afraid to trust Eddie due to his escaped from the hospital. Mullins did not need that. He wanted to know if he should give him a break. I told Mr. Mullins, "Please give Eddie a break." He was just like me, his father was dead, and he needed this. Mr. Mullins stated he would, but to give him time to see what he could do. However, he was very clear that at the first sign of a problem was all he needed to put our asses back. He was going to make arrangements to have us put on house arrest. We couldn't be seen anywhere other than the school. We had to complete a 26 student program. There were 13 teachers to meet us and who would teach us, to get us up to grade level. We would not have school breaks. Therefore, we had to work with other students in the same class in the fields with each other. Mr. Mullins asked if I understood. I said, "Yes sir, I understand," and from there things began.

## CHICKEN SCRATCH

✳✳✳✳

About three days passed and the police took us to the school and turned us over to Mr. Mullins' custody. Finally, Eddie and I were at the Pioneer school with 24 other misfits. We had to fight; it was the way of life. But we were defending ourselves. The ones that started it went to the boys' home the same day. So we knew we all had to be smart, by having a still tongue. The street law was to see and don't see, to hear and don't hear, but bear the code of silence.

Mr. Mullins' school system was the best thing that could have taken place in my life at that time. He changed my life forever, and to this day I thank him. Allow me to tell you how he operated. There were 26 of us most of the time and we had to work together. We would fight but Mr. Mullins would not find out about it. We could only put on the gloves and get in the ring we built, we were at play but at the same time we were at war. He would take us to the fields to pick tomatoes and use the money to take us on trips. He took us to places like the museum of art and science, to dinner where actors had lunch or dinner. He allowed us to meet people we'd never met with our parents. He took us to fish stocked bass ponds where I'd catch the fish and Eddie would clean them, Ivory cooked them and Calvin made fish sandwiches. We all had to rotate until everyone fed one another. Mr. Mullins gave us projects, like building radios from scratch with transistors to be put in place and building rockets. He gave me the opportunity to teach the art class every other Wednesday. All the fights stopped. We would still talk trash to one another, but we would not fight. We had learned to love and respect each other. Then one day the second stage of my life took place. Eli came to the school and went into the office and stayed for a long time. He was in there for more than three hours. When he came out he told me to get in the car. Mr. Mullins came to the car and said "John you are a real good young man; remember everything I taught you." He hugged me, and told me, "Goodbye and good luck. I got you put on probation." Somehow he set me free; I could not come back to the state of Michigan for five years. I was off to Baton Rouge, at age 14, the year of 1968.

My birthday April 21 1968, just a few days before Dr. Martin Luther King Jr. was killed. The city was put under curfew, a sea of blacks marched down to the capital and demanded a black flag fly equal to the flag, and of course there were problems. In the hood there wasn't a curfew. Before the riots broke, out an announcement over the radio told every house and business to tie a black scarf somewhere around it. It was intense in the city—there were no black crimes, no street fights, and every black person in the city was in one accord. We packed up our things and went to Florida. This is the third stage of my life. (Chicken Scratch) Did you read it?

We moved in with my mother's brother Elder Shanks. We picked fruit—after all, it is liquid gold. My uncles were dairy farmers. Uncle Earl Shanks, was a milkman; he milked cows. Uncle Elder was the mechanic. They both were good men. I was free, but I didn't know until mom, Eli, and Dorothy got ready to go back to Michigan.

I learned why Mr. Mullins and Eli took three hours to talk, and the reason Mullins said "remember what I taught you good luck." I found out what really happened, when mom told me not to write them and Eli said I could not call for the next 5 years; I couldn't be in touch with them. I was free. They told me "Fuzzy," that was my nickname, "don't get into anything;" and if I did, the police would come and take me back to jail. Mom said she was going to leave me with her brothers. She hugged me like she had never before, then she kissed me, looked at me and said she loved me. She told me to take care of myself and to work for what I wanted and that she would keep up with me. Earl, her brother, was our way of keeping in touch with each others lives. She said that we would see each other again someday. When our conversation ended they took off back to the great lake state of Michigan. (Chicken Scratch) Can you read it?

Here I am on my own; I have to do for myself. I am in the ninth grade and lost to the world. Man did I feel bad about how life looked for me, no one to call my own. What happened in my life that I got into such a mess? Somehow, thank God, I made it through this old tunnel of life.

Well, things did not work out with my uncles. They wanted to beat me along with their children. The problem was they beat them with a 2x6, five feet long. I told my uncle, "Not today," he told me to get out. So I got out, being back down in the south Rufus Robinson saw me and me being older, he told me that I could come stay with him and his wife Mrs. Alice Willis; she was a very nice person. But I really did not trust him. I needed to know if I still hated him because of the earlier years. I found that I didn't have any love in my heart for him, only hate. I soon found out that he hadn't changed. Rufus was the same in his heart and I heard him boast about how he once was. I got a job at the dairy as the Bogie Boy or Herdsmen. The bogie boy or herdsmen rounded up the cows to be milked inside the dairy by the milkmen. A dairy operates around the clock 24 hours a day; rain or snow, we worked for Norman Hales at Hales Dairy. I earned around $162.00 gross about $138.00 net and Rufus wanted $75.00 for my room and board every week plus $40.00 a week for food and $20.00 for laundry. That left me with $3.00, and he told me that if I did not pay, I had to go.

I caught a ride home with Mr. Bud Wright. It was raining so hard you could only see the front grill on the hood of the car. Mr. Wright's home was the third house on the line of the eight on the block. Rufus Robinson's house was the seventh house on the line. When we pulled up to the house there was a box soaked full of my few rags. Mr. Bud asked me "Are those your things." I answered, "Yes sir." He said, "Let's get out and get them and put them in the car." He got out as if the sun was shining and not raining. We both picked up the box. As we grabbed the box, it tried to come apart, but we managed to hold it together. Once we put the box in the car, we were soaked from head to toe, and we went to his house. It was still raining when he pulled up into the yard, and we got out of the car. He told me to come on, so we could get my stuff. We took the box onto the porch. He knocked on the door and his daughter Terrie answered. He said, "Tell your mama for you and her to fix up that room—this boy is going to live here with us." This is the fourth stage of my life.

My life as a free young man had just been placed into the hands of a man that I had no idea would have an impact on my life the way it did to this day. I thanked God for the people in my life and what changes I was about to go through. Until this day, I have never met anybody like these people. They were good people; God fearing people and would give you the very shirt off their backs. They'd go to church, stump the floor, shout and all, but would kill you as dead as a door knob, at the bat of an eye, if you did them wrong. I was in for the treat of a lifetime, and I found myself in love with the family. They took me in, when I say took me in, I mean just that, I was a part of the family as if I were their own son. They treated me that way. I remember after we had unloaded my things and I got moved into my room, I received a warm welcome from them. It was like I had known them my whole life.

Mr. Bud's full name was Alex Andrew Wright and Mama's name was Ellaphea; they had ten children; Zeek, Mae, Pre, Freddie, Janie, Carolyn, Papoo, Marry, Sonny, and Lil Man (aka Alex or Little Alex). They all took to me like a brother, even though I ended up married to Terrie, (Papoo). As this unfolds you will see how the relationship between me and Terrie developed. The day I moved in, Mr. Wright had a talk with me. He said, "Boy I am the man here; you eat what I eat. I eat gator tail, coons, and rabbits out the woods, turtles, and T-bone steaks. I wear blue Surd suits, and don't drive no other car but Cadillac's, and will bust a cap. You don't have to work anymore; you catch the bus to school right along with Papoo every day— now that is it, and you are at home here. I know you wonder why I am doing this don't you. I said, "Yes sir;" he said "Your granddaddy, I loved the ground he walked. He was the man I followed around in those woods from the age of 16. He got me drunk off the buck or home brew he made along with white lightning moonshine. He sold shine and I helped him move it from time to time. Your granddaddy was a hell of a fellow. I knew things about him that his own family didn't know. That is the reason that I am talking to you in this manner, to let you know that I don't play. I don't even play the radio." The look he had in his eyes told me he was no joke. He had two red stains on his white shirt. He had a spot on the left side above his heart and a spot on the right side next to his heart. Both spots were leaking from wounds of being shot five times with a ring nose four inch barrel 38. I went back to school for a while. I past to the tenth grade, went back later in life and got my GED, but from there I continued to live with the family. I felt at home, like a member of the family. We would go hunting, fishing and trapping. For the very first time I was starting to live my life. But everyday I thought about my sister Dorothy. I wondered about Eli and Mr. Mullins and how they set me free. It had to be something that Mr. Mullins saw in me. What?

Well I turned 15 and I asked "Papa"—that's what everyone in the family called Bud. He became "Papa" to me as well. I asked "Papa" if I could go to Georgia and visit my grandparents. Bud said I could go if I wanted to, but to come back because this is home.

I worked at the dairy a few weeks that summer and took off to Valdosta, Georgia. I met Barbie Smith my cousin's girlfriend from Indiantown, Florida. The place I had just left. She was staying with my grandparents while Willie was in Germany in the Army. She wanted me to meet her sister Mary. Barbie wrote Mary and told her about me so when I got back to Indiantown we could meet each other.

I stayed with my grandparents for the summer. Early one morning four boys came walking by the house cursing. My grandma said she had already told them boys about that nasty talk when they came around the house. So I yelled out to the guys for them to stop the cursing in the presence of my grandma—they kept on cursing. There was a pump BB gun in the house, I got it and shot one in the back of his neck, the other above the ear; I shot all them until they got out of range or off the road. That stopped the cursing, grandma came and took the gun from me and told me I could have hit one of them in the eye. I said, "Yes ma'am." While I was there, Rufus moved back to Georgia, said he wanted to see me, and he was going to give me the ass whipping I needed. So I went to Vallotton Dairy where he worked and hid outside the bay where he milked the cows to shoot him with a sawed off shotgun. Somehow God fixed it so that he was off that night and another man traded days off with him. I hated that man, but a day later in life I forgave him. I was just a child filled with a rage, put in me by him—hate from hate only equals hate. This man didn't even realize what he had done nor cared, but life turned on him. He felt worse than I could have ever felt, even when he would make me walk 10 miles through the woods on the blackest of nights, in the Georgia woods infested with snakes and wild animals, like black panthers.

**CHICKEN SCRATCH**

One followed me stopping when I stopped, every now and then. The panther stepped after I stepped and I could hear it as it walked on the dry leaves. I knew something was following me, so I would stand there for a minute out of fear. One Sunday evening, just as it was getting dark, my grandfather and I were on this dark lonely road walking. He told me not to step on anything black on the ground that I could see. I heard the thing walking on the leaves I asked my granddaddy if he heard the noise, he informed me that he did. I told him, I heard the noise every time I come down the road at night. Grand-daddy said "Do not run but to stay real close to me." Grand-daddy also said, to give him my hand, it didn't want him. It wanted me.

When we came to a running stream, a brook that crosses the road, we slowed down from the strong walk we were walking. All at once we heard something make a sound as it leaped across the brook and ripped the bark off the tree it went up. We heard it over our heads, and it let out this deafening scream as if it were no more than ten feet above our heads.

We didn't even speed up nor did we break our pace. We got down the road a little ways and granddaddy cut through the thicker part of the woods a path or a short cut to his house. We could hear this thing coming behind us, once we got to the house he told me to get inside. My grandma came to the door, asked granddaddy what was going on, he told her that something followed me through the woods. What it was, he did not know. Then we heard it when it turned around, it sounded like a bull going through the palmettos. Granddaddy didn't want them to ever send me over here at night again. That was a night that I would never forget—well, that was something I just had to mention.

Let me get back to the summer vacation, it was about over and it was time for me to go back to Indiantown Florida. I went downtown to buy my bus ticket but I ended up robbing a pool hall gambling game going back to what I was. I saw a young man I knew, his name was Henry Orr. I had him to give me a ride and someone had called the law. Now I'm running. I had to get back to Mr. Bud. I had at least $250.00 from the robbery so I bought a 50lb bag of coal for my grandparents, paid Henry to take the coal to them, and also had him to purchase my bus ticket for me. He did just that for me. I sat in his car until the Miami south bound Greyhound pulled into the bus station. I gave Henry $50.00 dollars and I did not tell him the law was looking for me. I left for Indiantown and that was the last crime I ever committed. My bus came in and I got on board, sat back in the seat, and gazed out of the window. As I passed through the city, I was wondering what mom, sis and Eli were doing.

# CHAPTER THREE

**MY LIFE WAS A MESS,** if I could just put this behind me and get this mess out of my blood. I needed a new mind and a new spirit, not realizing that was well on the way once I got back to Indiantown where this old man was. Somehow it seemed as if my mind stayed on him all the time; if it was not on mom it was on Bud Wright. (Chicken scratch)

It was something about Bud that just seemed right, I knew he was a very dangerous man and yet he was like a God sent man. Bud Wright and his family, in plain words, they were just real about life. I arrived in Stuart Florida twenty miles from Indiantown; Bud was at the bus station waiting for me. I had called earlier and notified him the time of my arrival.

## CHICKEN SCRATCH

They welcomed me back home and there I remained. My life changed 100%, a real turn around. We would go fishing and trapping. We would kill twenty-five rabbits or more. When we would fish, we would catch one hundred or more bluegill and largemouth bass. Momma Fee could cook, or as they say burn. She could cook any dish no matter what it was. She had a way she cooked wild food, and a way she cooked common food, either way it was good. I met Mary Smith, Bobbie Smith's sister, and we dated for almost a year. I thought we would end up getting married. But one day Terrie and I started talking to each other on another level. Although she was three years younger than me and I was 16 and she was only 13 years old, she made more sense on common ground than Mary Smith did. Mary was and still is a very good person, but she was not who God had for me. Terrie was the one it took for a person like me. Somehow I sensed that at a young age. So I stopped seeing Mary and stayed away from her. Terrie and I first became the best of friends we held respect for each other for three years. Bud let us know that it would be bad news if we violated that trust he put in us. During these three years, Bud got sick, we did not live on the line anymore, we moved to Booker Park.

We lived on the corner of 4th and canal St. in one of Mr. Howard's rental houses. We no longer worked for Norman Hales at the Hales Dairy, the reason we no longer lived nor worked there, was because one night Mr. Hales came to the dairy to spy on his help, to see if they were working. (Chicken scratch) Can you dig it?

He needed to see if any of his men were drinking on the job. Well, that night from the feed room a place where tons of feed for cattle is stored to feed the livestock. He saw a man named Mr. Jean Harris, in the diary, beating one of his cows with the end of a spray nozzle attached to the water hose and the cow was bellowing out. Mr. Hales could not take this man beating his cow like that so he ran out of the feed room into the dairy. Norman Hales stood six foot two and weighed 285 pounds. He was meaner than a junkyard dog. Poor Mr. Jean weighed about 155 soaking wet and stood about five foot four at the most. Mr. Hales grabbed Jean on the back of the neck, took the hose from his hand, and then beat Jean not like he was beating a child but like he trying to hurt a horse. He beat Jean's ass as if it were in the 1800s, when masters beat their slaves. Then he threw him to the floor and yelled, "Now milk them Goddamn cows." Jean hit the floor running the machines like a mad man, robots couldn't do like that. Then he looked for Big Benny Web who was a black man just as big as him, and did see him. He went and looked into the bathroom and found him asleep on the stool. Norman kicked him in the ass, off the stool; yelled, "Get your ass in there and milk them cows, you big sorry son of a bitch, get to it." Big Benny went without cleaning. Norman walked up and down the barn talking trash to all his workers, except for Zeek the one that took a man head off with a 12 gauge shot gun he just look at Zeek and said, "I'm not talking about you Zeek," but he knew if he would have started with Zeek all hell would have broken loose right there in the DAIRY. He walked up to Lil Man and said, "That go for you too," and pointed his finger in Alex's face and touched him. That was it, Norman Hales had to run for his life, he ran so, that he did not have the time to stop for his car—Little Alex was on him. He managed to get into one of his old trucks and run through fences and all trying to escape for his life; he had to go or die.

Well, Mr. Bud had missed all the action because he was the bogie boy out in the pasture, rounding up the cows to be milked. When Bud got to the dairy he wanted to know where little Alex was. Nobody was talking. He asked Zeek. Zeek told him that the last time he saw little Alex, he had Norman Hales stretched out and running for his life; and that Bud had better go get him. Bud quit right then and came home. We had to tie little Alex down with a rope all night long. Bud stayed up oiling his guns in a chair next to the front door so that he could see down the road both ways. (Chicken scratch) Well, daylight finally came, what a long night, good god where am I, never in my life until now did I understand that I was in a house of madness.

Everyone came down to Bud's house the next day about 8:30 a.m. to discuss what happened to Jean and Big Benny. Earl Shanks and Big Benny Webb were there; and as they were talking Norman drives up and he says, "What the hell is going on here." He says, "Benny go home." Big Benny went home. He told Earl to get in his car, Earl told him that he wasn't going anywhere and he meant it. However, momma told Earl to get in the car because he had nine kids and that we didn't have any room for all of them. She also told him to find a place as soon as he could and to get the hell off of Norman Hales' place. That time, Earl got in the car. Norman Hales called Bud's name, but that's as far as he got. Momma yelled, "Run man run." Bud reached by the door and grabbed his 12 gauge shot gun and shot at the car but Hales trail was blazing with dust. So Bud got a chair and a box of bullets and set by the door. So I asked momma, "Why is he sitting by the door like that?" She told me he was going to kill that man when he came by that morning, I asked her if she was talking about Mr. Hales. She told me that as soon as he comes by, because he has to come that way, and when he does, Bud is going to shoot him. I asked her, "Could he really do something like that?" She said he could. I asked her, "Could you stop him?" She stated to me that nobody could at that point, and for me not to go around him, not to say a word to him. Momma told me and Terrie to stay away from him because that was not the Bud that we knew. She said that she knew him and then she would walk and constantly say, "Calm down, Buddy boy, calm down." He did not seem to hear, (Chicken Scratch) What a day!

Suddenly, I heard the roaring of a car coming down the road, and it was Hales and Bud recognized it to be him, and when he got in range, Bud aimed at the car in passing. When he went to pull the trigger I grabbed the barrel and pushed it away from Hales' car as it passed. The gun fired, but it missed the car. Bud put the barrel of the gun under my neck, what in the hell have I done, with the barrel he pushed me against the wall then pushed me up the wall with the barrel until we were eye to eye, and he told me that I had better not ever do that shit no more. Mama told Buddy not to hurt me and to let me go. Then suddenly he let me drop to the floor, rushed to his room and slammed the door very hard. I did not see him until at least 7 hours—that is how long it was before he came out of the room. Things soon went back to normal. We packed up the furniture and moved that same day. I became attached to these people over the years. There were times they could make you laugh until water would flow from your eyes, the things they would do. (Chicken Scratch) can't understand it?

We went fishing in the St. Lucie River. It is brackish water, a man-made canal from Lake Okeechobee to the Atlantic Ocean, a mixture of salt and fresh water. This means some game fish like Snook would be available every spring, all along the river. However it was against the law to catch them out of season because Snook were game fish. Well, we were fishing with crawfish for catfish, when the game warden came up and started to ask for our fishing license and saw that Bud had caught a Snook. The Snook must have weighed around 8 pounds. He said, "I see you got yourself a nice Snook there. Let me see your fishing license, please sir, and that fish just cost you your right to fish, your automobile and your home, plus you are going to jail. You can put it back in the water and if it swims off everything will be ok, if not you have a problem." By then the officer had walked away from Bud and began to ask each one of us for our license, checked our buckets for the type fish we had, but Bud had the only Snook of the day. So he came back to Bud and when he got to where Bud was, the fish was lying across his legs. Bud was beating it on the side, then he would blow down the fish's mouth as if he were giving it mouth to mouth resuscitation and he was repeating this method. The game warden was shocked, he said, "What are you doing, sir?" Bud said, "I am blowing breath back in this mother fucker if it is going to cost me all this shit." Man I tell you the warden almost fell to the ground, he laughed until water flowed from both of his eyes. He said, "You can keep that one but do not catch anymore." He could barely get the words out without laughing. That ended our day of fishing I just had to mention that to show the type of a person Bud was. He was just real and just plain old Bud.

# CHAPTER FOUR

**AS YEARS PAST I GREW** even closer to the family. The role that Mr. Mullins and Bud played in my life seemed like it was planned in stages. Terrie and I got married, she was 16 and I was 19. We moved from the family home and got a small place of our own.

Before I get into this stage of my life, I would like to talk a little more about Bud Wright. As I lived with the family, the more I learned about the family. Mr. Bud was a low profile legend in his own time, a hard stone cut kind of a fellow. Mr. Bud was born in Adel, Georgia to Alex Andrew Wright and Channie Bleches. He lived most of his life in Valdosta. The stories I heard about Mr. Bud's life, came from his brothers, people who knew of him, and what Mr. Bud told me personally. His story started at a very young age, in a place where racism was bad and still is today. Valdosta, Georgia, a town founded in 1860 and the home of Doc Holiday and vigilantes of the south. The place where Mary Turner was hung upside down by her heel string and her unborn baby was cut from her belly. When her baby fell to the ground one of her killers took the heel of his boot and crushed the infant's head then riddled her body with bullets. This happened in 1918, months before Bud was born. For the next seven years our nation burned with hatred in the southern towns like Rosewood and others burnt to the ground. This is what it was like in the young years of Bud's life, the spirit breaking of the black man. Those that this system could not break created people like Bud at heart. Our lives, being unjustified in the eye sight of some unknown reason, even if we are forced to live under fear and stressful conditions, fueled by racial hatred, from as far back as 1829 before the revolutionary war that lead to the end of slavery. Thank God there were people like William Lloyd Garrison and Wendell Phillips that set the stages for the Bill of Rights. That states that the slaves ought to be instantly made free, and brought under the protection of the law. They made statements, like our fathers were never slaves, never bought and sold like cattle, never shut out from the light of knowledge and religion, never subjected to the lack of brutal taskmasters. Here 185 years later we are still going through the struggle for justice and equality. This was the tone of a nation when black people were gaining, in the world of a free society; the black renaissance. (Chicken Scratch)

The Black Renaissance and reformation was wiped out by murders on a large scale coast to coast. This was the atmosphere that Bud grew up in. Bud and I sat and talked about his life as a young man growing up in the south. He told me a story, about a time when he was 11 years old and being called names by a white boy. The boy called him all kind of names, like darkie and nigger, and the storekeeper allowed it.

Bud said he left the store, walked down the road, and hid in the bushes to wait for the boy. When the boy showed up, Bud jumped out in front of him and said, "It's just you and me, talk that shit now." Bud took his sling shot, loaded it with a large stone, pulled it back as far as he could. The Boy saw what Bud was going to do and he tried to run. Bud shot him in back of the head. The boy fell and blood ran out of him as if a main artery had been cut. Bud left him for dead, he thought. He said he didn't know he hit him that hard but he did.

Well, Bud went on home and did not tell anyone what he had done. In the meantime someone came along and found the young man on the road and took him to the doctor, which saved his life. The injured boy's father came and picked him up from the doctor. He asked his son what had happened. The boy told his father where the incident took place and what had occurred. So they rounded up a crew and headed for the country to see about the matter.

Bud's mother and father were sitting on their front porch and they heard a loud roaring of engines coming in their direction, not knowing these people were coming to take their son. The crew rushed up to the house. The father jumped out of the car with his son and said, "Preacher look

**CHICKEN SCRATCH**

at what one of your boys done to my boy," and, "We come for him." At that time Channie, Bud's momma stepped to the door with a double barrel shot gun, and told them that hell would freeze over first. Bud said guns came from every car and it was about 15 loads of them. (Chicken Scratch)

Old man Alex yelled out at Channie that he would handle the situation and for her to shut up. She said, Bishop, nobody was taking one of her boys. Old man Alex was a bishop and he managed to calm things down. Old man Alex said that "no one is going to take not one of mine nowhere." The man said, "We just wanted to whip his ass is all." Old man Alex said, "I will beat mine if anyone of them is guilty of knocking that hole in your boy's head. I will beat him and nobody else." The man called his son to identify the one that hit him. Bishop Wright called all of Bud's brothers they all lined up but Bud. In the line was Calvin, who we knew as Uncle Cal, James (Uncle James), Leroy (Uncle Leroy), Theodore as TB and Lee Andrew. The boy said that it was TB and he believed that it was him. Bishop told them that it could not have been him because he was with him in the field all day. The boy said, "It show look like the one that hit me."

Bud came from around the house and told them that he had hit the motherfucker. The boy then said that was him that hit him. The man jumped and said, "Did you hear that, he is a real hot head." The boy's father told Bishop that since he said he was going to whip his ass, "then let's get to it, and I mean get it now!" (Chicken Scratch)

That's the time the old man called Bud, looked him in the eyes, pulled him close to him and whispered into his ear. Bud said that he asked him if he sees what he has done. Then he had Bud to get down on the ground and he put his foot on his head and started beating him. Bud said that his daddy beat him and beat him until the man said that it was enough, but his father did not stop. The man yelled for him to stop hitting the boy, "not another damn time," because he thought he was going to kill him. Bud said that he did not let one tear fall from his eyes, instead he looked the man into his eyes the whole time his daddy beat him. I asked Bud how did it make him feel to have his father beat him for another man's command. He told me that, that was a time of hate. The black man hated the white man because of shit like that. The white man hated the black man because,

## CHICKEN SCRATCH

they had lost their slaves. Nobody was going to work their asses off for free, and he hated that shit. Besides the fact that they knew we didn't have any rights at all, they could do anything to us and get away with it by the law. There was no constitutionality in this land for any blacks, especially in the south. (Chicken Scratch)

Looking at life in America today; very little has changed, it's only more complex. There are many stories about Bud Wright, like he shot his uncle and the son at the age of 17. Bud said it was early one morning.

They were working at this warehouse where a white man had a feed company for livestock, and Bud was a bagger. A bagger was a person who, when the sack was full of feed, he sealed the opening of the bag, and took it into another room for storage. Bud said he was a big, tall, young man weighing around 225 to 235. Being mostly lean, and he could take two 100 lb. bags into the storage room at a time with one under each arm. Well, Bud's uncle wanted him to carry one bag at a time. Bud refused to do so, and his uncle got very upset and demanded that he carry one bag at a time. Bud's uncle started to curse at him badly. He told Bud he was the boss, and damn it do it like he wanted it done. Bud told him he wasn't doing shit and he was going to keep doing it the way he had been doing it. His uncle left Bud alone, but the son heard the way Bud was talking to his father. He went in to get on Bud about talking to his father that way.

Bud said that's when he reached over and got his single shot shotgun and shot his cousin in his ass. He blew all the ass out of the seat of his cousin's pants. Bud said his cousin got his ass the hell out of the feed room then. Bud said, "My cousin telling me about how to not talk to his dad that way, I gave him the treat of his life!" His uncle eventually saw his son all down on the ground rolling around in the dirt yelling, "Bud shot me, Bud shot me." Bud's uncle ran into where Bud was and said, "You shot my boy!" Bud aimed the gun at him, his uncle turned to run out of the room, but it was too late. Bud blasted him the same way he blasted the son, now they both were rolling around in the sand yelling, "Bud shot me," to the boss man. When the boss man came in the feed room where he was, he was working like nothing had happened.

## CHICKEN SCRATCH

The man asked him what happened. He said, "They came in here fucking with me and I shot them in the ass."

Bud Wright was a character all the days of his life. He was a legend in his own time, a black man determined not to be broken. A few other stories was that Bud Wright beat a man pants off of him with a 2x4, beat a white man down downtown in front of the courthouse in Valdosta for ripping the clothes off a black woman. Bud had supposedly buried a white Federal Agent alive regarding a shine still. Bud's boss was a white farmer; Bud lived on his farm as a sharecropper and worked for him for three years. As a result of Bud not having an education, the farmer took Bud's money from the crops for two years. The farmer tried the same thing the third year and Bud beat him with a hammer until he almost killed him. As a result, Bud and his family had to leave Valdosta in the fear of being killed. After all, this was the same place that Mary Turner was murdered.

The same place that Sidney Johnson was killed and then tied to the back of a pickup truck in May of 1918, on the South Side of Valdosta, and his body was drugged up and down

Patterson's street and then 40 miles to Morven, GA. This was the man that took me in at the age of 14. I could not believe the things I was hearing. But after I began to look into things I found them to be true, what a life. I must stop about Bud because that is another book; it will take a book and time to tell his story of those days. The man I knew was a hard old man but a very good person, you just did not piss him off and if so, he would act up real bad. I need you to understand my reason for mentioning Bud the way that I did. See all these people God put in my life were building me for the storm of my life for the rest of my life.

God knew I needed what they instilled within, to fight with faith, to endure and how to seek refuge under God's wing as a shelter from the storm. This is the transition of the story about the life I asked God for, on the night I lay on the trailer gazing into the midnight blue sky, looking upon the stars.

As I had stated, Terrie and I got married on October 14, 1973. Our oldest son was born January 27, 1973. Here I am with a son, another person like me. He was my pride and joy. He changed me. I did not have the education I needed to get a really good job. But I knew how to pick oranges and that's what I did until I found a job as a grove tender. It was a job with no future.

Where am I? I must do something that will make a difference in all of our lives, because I am the one that is the head, or classified as head of household even by the IRS. It is going to take courage to make the trip of a lifetime. As I sit here at 2:31 a.m. in the morning looking back, I really have a view to recall the review. At this point I feel, before I continue, there is something I need to do so that the reader can understand the reasons and will of the mind of a man trying to tell the story of his life. A man that has been diagnosed with a terminal Esophageal Cancer, with the life expectancy of five years from the time diagnosed. I am that (Chicken Scratch) can you read it? Cancer was found in me on March 8, 2008. It had grown and wrapped around my stomach and esophagus like a tree root system. The doctor said it had grown there for over twenty years.

Life has been a struggle for me and it looks like it will be that way all the way to the grave, yet I am holding on to something. What is it? Why the will? Please help me find the answer, read the scratch if you can. Getting back to the story of my life as I seek for reason. Terrie and I were proud young people, we were alive, we had to live and we had just reproduced another, to combat this world. Neither of us knew what life was at the time. Maybe we took it to be a bed of roses. Not knowing the thorns of life would distort the picture or point of view we had as young people, to live happily ever after. Our little raggedy house was a seasonal camp house apartment. These units were built for the migrant lifestyle. The broader line of living above or below the line of poverty at all times. Our rent was $25.00 a week. The minimum wage was around $3.00 per hour or less. When you hear the words...the blind can't lead the blind, that is a true fact. Black people were not sight blind, but were blinded by what they were not exposed to, nor permitted to see knowledgeably or mindfully. Therefore, we were blind like Malcolm said; "Hoodwinked and bamboozled." Me and Terrie and now Tyrone, our son was born into this mess of a system. As parents we had to make a way for his future, and we didn't even have one of our own. We were two people married in the heat of the struggle. We truly believed this was the LIFE, living the struggle, by the struggle, produce by the struggle. (Chicken scratch)

The place we lived was called Rogers Quarters, the apartment that we rented was a long single building with 8 units. Each unit was a front room, bedroom, toilet, kitchen, and that was it. In the front of the place was this dirt street with rain water washouts, or craters—some were deeper than others. Terrie's job was staying at home with the little one. She would work from time to time, not that she had to, but she would, to help out. We were a real team. I would drink a beer only on the weekends, none through the week. Well, time moved on; we grew older. I got a job working for Coca Cola. They had just purchased Minute Maid orange groves in Florida. Working for Coca Cola, I experienced on the job discrimination in the early 1970's. I did not have a trade; not skilled enough for grove work, other than picking oranges, or fruit from the trees and vines. But I did learn to operate light weight equipment which was no more than tractor driving. (Chicken scratch)

I felt a little pride because I felt like I had moved up in life. I'm making a little more money. I'm dreaming about getting us a home, or a better place to live. Ah man, I had this I'm moving up spirit. I'm working for the Coca Cola food division. I have a chance to work my way up through opportunity, I thought. At this same time, I had won a scholarship with the art instruction school and with Palmer Writers. It was a correspondence course I took for several years in commercial art. I was trying all that I could to gain ground for a better living. I was young and didn't really know which way to go, but I did know I wanted to become something in life. I knew that I was not going back to where I came from, and getting this job with Coca Cola was an out. I reported to work at track-b. The grove was divided into two sections; one side was track-a and the other side was track-b. There was a wide canal from the St. Lucie River for irrigation that separated the two tracks. Each track was hundreds of acres of orange groves. I worked directly for James Bush, who was the superintendent of track-b.

Early one morning while doing my job, which consisted of servicing equipment, checking water in the radiator, oil and lubricating all the fittings on a water truck used to water young newly planted orange trees, Mr. James Bush walked over to me. In his hand he held a book. He said, "Hey Johnny let me show you, what all a nigger is good for." He said this so everyone in the shop could hear him make what he thought was funny. (Chicken Scratch)

Everyone was shocked. There were only four other employed blacks besides myself of the 17 employees on track-b. James Bush took this nasty book which had a black man's face down between a white woman legs on one page, and the same black man leaning back with the woman's body part between his teeth, stretched as far back as he could lean. Everyone in the shop just stopped as if they were frozen. I could not believe this man did that, it was unreal.

I asked him if I could take off for a couple hours. Told him I had to go take care of something. I went to the nearest phone and called the President of the Coca Cola foods division—his name was Mr. Bill Middlebrooks—at first I could not get through to talk to him. Once he understood the nature of the call, he immediately got on the phone with me. I told Mr. Middlebrooks what had just taken place out on the grove, and that I was going to take other steps. He asked me to give him a chance, and that a man by the name of Jack Norris would be there to see me the next work day.

Mr. Jack Norris was the president for the Florida division of Coca Cola Foods. At 7am the very next day, at track-a where we all report in for work, a white car came rolling into the yard with this long whip antenna on the back. I knew who this had to be. I said to myself, "That's the man that's going to get equilibrium around this place."

Sure enough, he made everything stop that was in motion on the job and called a meeting right then and let it be known he was about to conduct an investigation about an allegation made, charging discrimination. No one, other than Mr. Norris and myself, knew about the allegations. Soon after the meeting started, people began to act as if they were from another planet when it came to the issues of what happened the day before. The people from track-a didn't know what happened, but some had heard what had taken place.

## CHICKEN SCRATCH

It is strange, how whenever people can do something, they seem to look more toward the physical existence and their dependence upon material things, than the highest principles of life, their bill of rights pertaining to Justice and Equality by the law. (Chicken scratch) Do you feel me?

As the investigation took off, questions were being asked for the very first time from the very top of Coca Cola Food Division about the treatment of the people. It was the seal lip thing of the moment, but they wanted to talk. You could feel the intensity in the air that if just one person could spark the talks, then everyone else would open up. Well, two ladies stepped up to the plate and told what had happened at track-b—this got things on the move. The Farm Workers Union was already there. Some of the people were angry with me because I didn't go to the union about what took place at track-b. Why should I go to the Union? The Stewart was the one giving out the obscene literature including the book Mr. James Bush showed me. It worked out that it took three weeks of investigation, and finally the last day, or the big show down was about to happen. I believe that it was on a Friday, the last meeting was called and Mr. Jack Norris was about to do his thing as the power of change.

Well, the meeting began. There was this long table in the room and Mr. Norris was sitting at the end. He asked me to sit next to him on one side of the table and for Mr. James Bush to sit on the other side. The other foreman and key witnesses took their seat around the table, and others filled the seats in the room. Once everyone was in the room, Mr. Norris started talking. He stated we all knew he was conducting an investigation pertaining to a charge or allegation made against one of their superintendents of this division, Hudson Grove, over the past few weeks. He stated the incident occurred at track-b and the charge was by Mr. John Robinson, a light equipment operator. (Chicken scratch)

Another foreman had a secret witness to come in to testify that she did not see the book, and I was lying about that morning. She stated she was in the shop and that the incident didn't happen. Mr. Norris, in regards to everyone he spoke to during his investigation, stated he believed that I was being truthful. He turned to me and said he was there to set things straight and it would happen before the meeting was over. Mr. Norris went further to say, Mr. Bush had been working at Hudson Grove for years and Mr. Bush and had never done anything like the incident, to his knowledge. He also publicly noted that Mr. Bush and I had worked at the company side by side. However, Mr. Norris wanted me to know that Mr. Bush's job was in my hands. All I had to do was say the word and Mr. Bush could lose his job on the spot. I looked across the table at Mr. James Bush and then around the room. I directly looked in the eyes of Mr. Bush and told Mr. Norris, I passed Mr. Bush's house every day and saw his children standing along the roadside waiting for the school bus. I saw the holes in their shoes and their clothes. I knew that Mr. Bush didn't have the education for the position he holds, but his time on the job spoke to his training. I told them that no, I didn't want to see him fired, even though I should. I just wanted equality at Hudson Grove. A man named Milton spoke. He was one of the other foremen who spoke up for Mr. Bush. Milton tried to justify Mr. Bush and the book. He tried to say that I had put myself in the position to be called a name or to be spoken to in that manner. Mr. Norris asked me if I understood what Milton was saying because he certainly didn't. I asked Mr. Norris if he thought I would put myself in a position to be called a nigger. I told Mr. Norris, "Do you see that lady sitting near the door? I caught Mr. Milton on top of her just banging away in the company truck and I mean the company truck was rocking. It had rained very hard and the block of groves where I found them in the act was where it was very easy for a pickup truck to get stuck. On my passing along the road, I saw the truck down in the grove, I stepped off the tractor. In fear of getting the tractor stuck, I walked inside the grove. When I was near the truck, I heard this noise. It was her. I saw the door open on one side with both her heels up and him on her. Then I went back to my tractor and came to the shop." I asked Mr. Norris how Coca Cola would feel if they read the headlines and it read "grove worker killed by officer of the law on grove site." Because the woman near the door is married to a police officer. So no, I would never put myself in the position to be called a nigger, and everyone there knew I was telling him the truth. There was no way I would ever put myself in a position to be called a nigger. I

## CHICKEN SCRATCH

mentioned to Mr. Jack Norris that he said he was going to get things right and I expected justice. I told him to let Mr. Bush keep his job. I just wanted it so we all could have a better place to work. We loved our families too, and we had to work some place. Milton was fired on the spot, James kept his job, the only boss I had was Mr. Norris. I later transferred to picking oranges, then soon quit. (Chicken Scratch) Did you get it?

The union was on the job, but it was on Coca Cola's payroll. All the people dues came out of their pay checks each week. You could be a union member or not a member. The reason I transferred was the long term get back, in my heart and mind I could sense that if I stayed I didn't have a chance. Sooner or later, I would be fired for some reason or another. See the union was against me and the company was afraid of me, because I would speak out against wrong policies defended by the union. The social game they played with the workers when it came to human and Civil-Rights—such as, they were using untested, long term proven, unsafe chemicals that were dangerous to human health. More people got cancer from that grove because of that reason.

The use of untested chemicals and the long term side effects were never expressed in a manner that a person would really know how dangerous those chemicals were to their health on a long term life scale. The use of Paraquat, a chemical compound used as an herbicide to kill weeds, this chemical had the potential to paralyze. Many employees died from cancer from the grove. (CHICKEN SCRATCH) You can't understand it. The union organized labor to save the company from lawsuits. They all were corrupted, in bed together, to screw the earnest working MAN, all because of that liquid gold "ORANGE JUICE."

The one on the bottom of the pole in society, the underprivileged or the poor lame duck, that pond is never full enough to make ends meet. (Chicken SCRATCH) What was that?

I tried to make up my mind to stay. I just couldn't. And besides, I didn't see what I was looking for. I thought I did, but I found it was not there. I had a part time job at a ranch plowing land, thousands of acres. So I went to work there part time until I could find a better job. I went to work for modular homes, and they trained me for six months as a trim carpenter, then to operate the saw shop. There I learned a trade. Now I feel like I'm finding myself, just as things was looking up for me, the company went under—back to my part time job. The guy that ran the job on the ranch was named Marvin. Marvin worked from a strict budget that was why my work was part time. He would allow me to work more if the sales were good and budget reflected. The ranch was a non-profit tax shelter; any money made had to go back into the ranch. It was owned by Olin the owner of Winchester. They had a bird farm and hunters would come out there to hunt, these were big shots. One day I went over to help out at the bird farm. They were burning off the underbrush which had fire lanes cut by a bulldozer. I was given a pine top or limb to beat out any fire that jumped the fire lane to keep fire from spreading and setting the other fields on fire that were not to be burned.

It was a very hot and dry day. Around 3pm, I had to stop and take a break, so I just stood still, as a cool breeze of air passed. As I looked down, next to my feet was this 6-foot long, diamondback rattlesnake. I don't know how, but I jumped about 8 feet from the place I stood. An old white man that gave me the limb heard me calling to him. When he came, he asked me, "Boy what is your problem other than the fact that your ass don't want to work."

I got very angry and I told him that there was a big Diamondback Rattlesnake over where I was working. He called me a liar and said that my sorry ass just didn't want to work and told me to show him where the "snake" was. He had a mouth full of tobacco, I mean a mouth full. I saw the snake, but he did not see it, and I was hoping that it would bite him. So I told him the snake was in a spot next to the palmettos, but it was next to his feet. When he leaned over to see where I told him the snake was, the snake struck at him with such force that it had hit a palmetto leaf which caused the snake to miss his face by inches, this thing struck like lighting. The man grabbed his neck as though he was bit, but he was choking from all that tobacco in his mouth, even his color was changing as he struggled to regain his breath. When I saw his reaction, I couldn't help but laugh.

Well, I just walked out of the woods to my car and went home. Terrie commented that I was home early and asked me what happened. I told her it was a long story, that I almost stepped on a large Diamondback Rattlesnake and that I had quit my job. I didn't know what I was going to do, but I would find me a full time job. My part time work at the ranch was over and I had filled in at the bird farm for that day.

Later that night, there was a knock at the door. A guy by the name of Robert Willis, asked me if I still wanted the job at the juice plant. If I did, then I had to arrive at the plant the next morning. This would be a new beginning for me and my family. That night I told my wife that I had a job at the juice plant, and we wondered what kind of work I would be doing there. I had heard they were training people for positions. The only trade I had was carpenter skills. The next day, I reported to the plant to fill out the application. I started as a laborer from the bottom; I was trained as an extractor operator. It didn't take me long to learn the operation.

There were nine extractors on each line and there were two lines for a total of 18 machines. These are juicers, they cut the oranges and the juice was extracted by a vacuum suction line at the bottom side of the cutter cup. I would like to express and define the complete operation but the complexities of the many aspects of the plant are too great. It would take another book to define the complete operation. But I will say, when I walked through those doors I saw another world, a new life, I thought, eureka. This was just what I had been looking for, a brand new start. I went with dedication, gave all I had, and that was my labor, mind and spirit. I would fill in if any person was laid out for work. The only times I would not fill in, were for the jobs I had not been trained.

One morning, I was asked if I would be willing to learn everything about the plant so that I could be the person, what they called a Swingman, which is a person that fills in for a person that doesn't report to work. My heart pumped up with joy, man I had done it. I found my hope again. I was about to learn a host of skills. I would be able to feed my family, provide a future for them from my hard work and a willingness to put them first. I would do this for them. Because God gave me the new life I asked for, here it was.

**CHICKEN SCRATCH**

Who would've believed me if I told them about what's taking place in my life at this point. (Chicken scratch) Defined.

# CHAPTER FIVE

**I WAS A YOUNG MAN** searching for a life. There was something in me, and it must be in my genetics, because I am being driven from within to have something. I knew I had to work for it; I knew that. So, I went at it with all I had. They trained me as a blender, to blend juices in large amounts like 3000 gallons at a time for shipping; to operate a Taste Evaporator, cooking the juices, removing the water, concentrating the juice; to measure the brix, which is the amount of sugar by concentration. For example a customer would place an order for 5 to 1. This means 5 parts of water to 1 part of concentrate, whether it is by a gallon or a pint. I was trained to be a bin operator, fruit grader, electrician, welder, pipe fitter, peel bin operator, dryer operator, and last, an industrial mechanic. I became top of the line in the feed mill. As you see, I started from the bottom. At this point, years passed, about four in fact. During these four years my eyes were open to an environment that I really didn't believe was out there. I thought that what I was seeing was only at Coca Cola Minute Maid. I just couldn't believe it.

I started at the mill on the peel bins. The bins were containment units or holding bins for cut orange peels to be cooked into a byproduct then compressed into pellets by a machine called a Pelletizer for shipping. The peel is transported by screw conveyors into a set of cutters called hammer mills. The chemical lime is then administered into the peel in order for the peel to be squeezed. The peels are then conditioned inside of a reactor screw or screws. From there, the peels go into other screw conveyors, and to presses that remove the liquid from the orange peel. Then to the dryer to be cooked and molasses added.

I was the only black man that worked at the mill when I first started there. It allowed me to express the type things I experienced early in the mill, and the type of people I worked for. As I said, I was on the peel bins. This mill was nasty, I mean nasty. Fires were burning out back where they were throwing feed away because they could not sell it due to the moisture content. The dryer was just running. Wet peel, mud, and maggots was on the yard of grass. It was bad, and the dust was out of control. Like I said, I was the only black man working at the mill. I became "boy clean this," or "clean that." I was the only person doing the cleaning for the two 12-hour shifts. I'd work 14 hours a day shoveling feed without a break, speaking to no one, I just shoveled feed. (Chicken scratch)

The juice plant was a seasonal operation. It operated only seven to eight months out of the year. That meant people got laid off every summer. I never got laid off because I worked hard. I was working for a reason and a cause. I had to have it. I was not going back from whence I came. That life was gone as I look back from where I sit now. This old life has been a rough and rugged road of sad and happiness. To sit here with cancer and try to write the story of my life, I guess, is the story of my life. Oh God, where am I? I know I have feelings, but where are they? In my heart, or just in my mind? What happened was that I was lost from within. Or was I just searching for that which I lost?

Yes, I worked at that plant and it gave birth to a new creature being hurt by the destiny of doom. As this cancer flows through my body, I still feel the same just the pain is physical. When, at one time, it was only mental stress from a beat down of an overworked body, from trying to make something happen. I have always known things don't just happen. You have to make them happen. (Chicken Scratch) Read it if you can.

I recall working with Homer Caldwell, a bigot, he was the maintenance superintendent, and I asked him if he would teach me to become a mechanic. I washed his tools, carried his tools, put away his tools, and yet he would say, "Johnny, look, we are the only two niggers here today," if we were working on something nasty and we were the only ones working that job. Yes, he would ask me if I could help him to get him some nigger pussy. He was a drunk, a real drunk, but he had the job. The thing was, I had to learn from this drunk. He was good, one of the best in the field of mechanics in the industry. I hated the conditions, but my ambition to learn the trade pushed aside the negativity, and also I learned people. I would hear Homer, and at times I'd say, "Look man, I do not want to hear that shit today," and he knew I meant it, because he would not use the word anymore. It was his teachings that helped me to rebuild that feed mill every year. As I reflect back, in the making of a new mind, I emerged from poverty to change my lifestyle for a lifetime. Hoping, in search of a rainbow, for that pot of gold, not this bag of sorrows. (Chicken Scratch) Don't read it.

When I first learned to operate the feed mill, a young man named Paul taught me. The reason was because Paul's girlfriend came to the job site one night, and he wanted her to think that he was the boss. So he came and got me and said, "Tell her I'm your boss." I let Paul's girlfriend know that I took orders from him, that he was the boss at the mill. The next night when we were on the night shift, I told Paul that was a good looking girl he had the night before. I mentioned to Paul that he ought to teach me how to run the mill. That way he could leave and I would cover for him while he was gone. He told me that Wayne, his boss, the one that hired the both of us, told him not to teach me how to run the mill. I asked him why, since they had trained me for all the other positions, why not this one? Paul proceeded to tell me what Wayne said. Wayne explained to Paul that Mr. Caulking didn't want no nigger to run the plant or the feed mill. "Wow!" I said. However, Paul told me that he would teach me what he knew, but that I really couldn't run it. In time, I kept it going longer than anyone else. By me shoveling feed all the time, I already knew Paul could not operate the mill. But he knew how to start it up and shut it down.

From the unit reactions, I noticed certain things would happen each time the temperature dropped. This only happened if the lime ran out for any reason, or the shoots that fed the presses plugged and the peel would bypass the presses thus entering the dryer without the water being removed. So Paul began to teach me how to start up the mill, and shut it down. I would make sure that the lime didn't run out and the shoots to the presses did not bypass and the brix in the molasses stayed high. What I am saying is that I learned what created the problems that led to the major problems. All I had to do was make sure that this did not happen by allowing the peels not to be limed down in the reactor conveyor before it entered the dryer. Therefore, the first amount of feed sold was cooked by me, but Paul got the credit for the product. It could not be known that I could operate that mill. So I became a shadow operator. (Chicken scratch)

They boasted on how Paul was running the mill. They even gave him a big raise. I never found out how much his raise was. But Paul said it was as much as all the other foremen working at the plant. Well, I kept the mill running. The other shift was unproductive completely. The mill was still a mess because it would be down most of the night and the peels would be what we term as sour or fermented. This caused the lime to not create the reaction needed for the liquid to be removed from the peel, which caused a slower operation for the drying process. The feed mill was at the end of the juice plant operations. That meant only one thing, the plant had to stop its operations, because the holding bins for the peels were full.

## CHICKEN SCRATCH

The plant and the feed mill were two different operations. Each had its own facility. The juice plant had a tank farm with ten or more 80,000 gallon tanks for concentrated orange juice and the feed was for animals. When the feed mill went down the juice plant had no place for its peels. If the mill was down or the plant stayed down for long periods of time, that meant that the pickers in the field would have to stop picking. The entire operation would cease operating. Anyway, one shift was productive and the other was not. The only productive shift was the one I was running. Now take a look at what I went through as a young black man. I had to become a shadow of the day in the day. I felt like a drowning man grasping for a straw. I needed something to hold on to other than my hat. (Chicken scratch)

The other problem was that the operators on the other shift drank on the job. There are some things I need to clarify in order for you to have a clear understanding of things that happened; which I know for a fact changed things for me. Paul had a twin brother and they really loved one another.

When you would see one, you would see the other. If you didn't it would not be long before the other one would show up. We were working the night shift around four o'clock a.m., when Paul came to me saying he had not heard from his brother. He knew that something was wrong. They had never been this far apart. Well, he stayed as long as he could. Then he took off about 15 minutes before his shift ended and left me there. I found out later that day, Paul could not find his brother. He drove 20 miles to Stuart Florida from Indiantown, Florida to see his brother's girlfriend. She told him he had went back home to Indiantown. Paul told her he didn't make it home. Paul started back to Indiantown and he traveled the route they usually traveled. Along the way he saw where a car had left the road just before a bridge that led to the St. Lucie River.

He saw what appeared to be something white below the water. He found it to be his brother's car. He went and pulled his brother's dead body out onto the top of the car which was about a foot and a half beneath the water. When the fire department arrived, they found a young man holding the body of the other on the top of the car. Paul found his brother. The paramedics had to put him to sleep just to get his brother out of his arms. Paul was from New York. The family had the body shipped back there. Paul and I had worked together and he came to see me. He stated he had to go, and would not be coming back. He couldn't live in Indiantown and not see his brother here with him. Being as close as they were they had never been apart. Paul just had to leave. As he was speaking, water was streaming from his eyes, but his voice had no tremble. He sounded like nothing was wrong, but I saw the pain in the tears. Paul was hurting inside. (Chicken Scratch)

Well, here we go. As you know, Paul taught me how to start and shut down the mill, even though he could not operate the mill on a consistent basis and keep it on line—just ran wet feed, a product no company would buy. That is where I came into the picture. I operated the mill from behind the scenes, as a shadow operator, and produced a byproduct fit for market. So no one other than Paul knew I could operate this mill. I mean, no one in management knew. There were only two 12-hour shifts. Paul ran one and Mack ran the other. The mill was now going back to the mess it was in. Paul was gone at this point. Paul went back to New York. That left me with these other guys, and to them my name was boy. That meant, John Robinson did not do anything to prevent the mill from running bad. Mack and the crew was now on the night shift and they drank every night. The mill was a real mess.

Feed was burning all out back. Then, two weeks after Paul was gone, during the night, the mill caught fire and the dust collector and the cooler burnt down. Well, as I was on my way in, I met Mack. He stopped me and told me to clean up some of the mess by the furnace. I agreed to do it, knowing that the president of the company was on his way out there. Mack wanted me to move the whiskey and beer bottles and cans out of view from the president. They kept them from coming to the mill, stalling to give me enough time to clean up the mess. But I took the whiskey that was in the bottles and poured it all over the floor and on the counter tops. I took a 55 gallon drum full of empty beer cans and dumped them all over the floor, then kicked them around. Then I walked toward them. As I passed Mack, he asked if everything was okay, I replied I got everything ready for you the

## CHICKEN SCRATCH

way you asked. Everybody got fired, but me, from the mill. (Chicken scratch)

Now panic breaks out and they do not have an operator for the shifts. Paul was the main man and Mack was the other, and the mill was a mess. We rebuilt the cooler and rebuilt the dust collector in two days around the clock working. When it came to the mill getting back on line, a young man named Bryant that worked with Paul, knew how to start the mill. Paul was teaching him to be his assistant operator and not me, orders of management. They put Bryant on the night shift, and then they told me not to touch anything in the mill. All they wanted me to do was to watch the place and not put my hands on anything. The mill was running. Wayne Thomas told me that he wished I knew how to run the mill. He told me that he would, if he could give me a chance to operate the mill.

I told him that I could run the place. He looked at me in the strangest way and said, "Do you really think you can run this mill?" I said, "Yes, I can." He turned around and laughed as if that was funniest thing he heard in awhile.

He said, "If you think you can run this place, you just do what we told YOU. Don't touch anything until we can get some one HERE. We got a man coming from another planet, and he will show all of us." Well, that day an electrical storm came and shut the plant down five times every twenty minutes. It was raining and storming so bad, if you were not at the mill, you could not get there. Once the storm was over, everyone came running to the mill. When they got there, they found the mill on line, running like it did when Paul was there. Palmer, the general manager, asked, "Did the power go off?" I told him that the power did go out. He asked, "Did you restart the mill?" I said, "Yes." I also informed him that the first feed you sold from back here, I ran. The general manager said, "I know you can run the evaporator. So keep running the mill. This is your shift. You just got a raise."

There was a complete turnaround in the mill from that point forward. I began to train people on how to run the mill as I had learned. When the season went down, I had men trained enough to keep the operation going, and progress was being made. I cleaned the mill up over the summer and made improvements that made the mill operate better.

## CHICKEN SCRATCH

I modified and built a lime conveyor dispenser. We became a team in the mill. But Wayne Thomas hated black people. There were so many times Wayne would do things to make my job hard to bear. In 1976, a man named Virgil Mills was a carpenter at the plant, and he was Wayne's best friend, and he wanted to be the superintendent over the mill. Virgil did not care about me being out there, he just wanted the mill. So one night, just after dark, Mr. Mills came out to the mill with his car lights turned off. I saw him as he approached. He got out of his car and sneaked inside, or so he thought. A newly hired young man named Lorenzo Edwards and I were resting from cleaning the floor from the mess the other shift had left. While we were standing there, Virgil walks up and he said, "That's why this place is in the shape it's in, because you guys standing around with your fingers up your asses. I am going to see Wayne in the morning, and Johnnie your ass is gone." I told him that I didn't give a damn. He could go tell who ever in the hell he wanted to tell. (Chicken scratch) Could you read that?

The next day when I reported to work, there they were, together, watching me as I passed through the plant. It wasn't long before Wayne made his way to the mill. He asked me if there were any problems at the mill or "were there any problems last night?" I told him there were no problems at the mill, and, "I do not work for Virgil Mills. I thought you, Wayne Thomas, was the production manager and that I worked for you." Then I informed him that Virgil wanted to be superintendent of the mill. I told Wayne Thomas that he had a major position, Palmer's got his position, and Virgil did not get a position like they did, and he wants the mill so he could feel big. The very next day, Virgil came to me and apologized for what he had done. Then he dropped the bomb he came to drop. He wanted to know if I'd work for him. He said that Wayne told him what I said about positions, and that I was right. But the only way he could get the job—I had to agree to work for him. I told Virgil the company didn't belong to me. It belonged to a man called George Caulking and it didn't matter, "go for it. I just need a job." Virgil told me he would get me a raise and I would become his head operator. He even stated that I could work in maintenance to get more hours. He got the position. I could see that he was proud of himself, but he could not see that

**CHICKEN SCRATCH**

I was hurt, from being the victim of discrimination again. For him to rise and for me to fall was a blow to me, but I had to stay there, because the mill seemed to be teaching me about it from its reactions.

A black man in this southern part of the country just could not get any justice, no matter what. Wayne Thomas didn't even consider the facts, that Virgil didn't know anything about the mill. Virgil had worked in the mill before, and just could not operate it. He knew a little, but not enough to maintain a constant smooth operation. Plus, he drank a lot of alcohol. I recall one night after he became superintendent he got so drunk, and we could not find him. He had passed out and somehow got under the center of his truck. We pulled him out and put him into the cab. There he stayed for about five hours. Then he just left. That's what I worked under and got skipped over for, but my mind was on greater things than the Virgil's of the moment. Knowledge of the mill and its function was my interest.

I was becoming part of the dryer system, a part or device as a functionary mind of the equipment. Therefore, I could not allow the Wayne's and Virgil's of the world to alter my goal and ability to learn. I knew on the top side of my trades this was the one of them all, to understand the art of the science of production. To understand this was just no common job.

# CHAPTER SIX

**AS I TRAINED PEOPLE, PERFORMED** repairs, and rebuilt the mill using and teaching trades, like welding, pump refurbishing, gearbox rebuilding, and a host of other skills relating to this dryer system, I had become good, in fact, one of the best. The way that I would practice welding is, I would weld for hours everyday, tig and stick welding. As a result of practice, I got certified by Transeastern, the company that did the Alaskan pipeline, and I got certified by the state of Georgia and Florida department of transportation 1-6-g, all the positions in welding. (Chicken scratch) check that out!

I would take a gearbox home with me from the mill scrap yard. I'd take that gearbox apart, and put it back together over and over, time and time again, until I could rework the unit by feeling of the parts. I didn't have to look at the part to tell where it needed be located on the gearbox. Knowing every part of the mill this way, gave me the edge I needed as to down time, and its functions. I was trained by the Honeywell Company to repair, install, and calibrate the sensitivity of the big dryer, and I was ready. This was a modular furnace, meaning it modulates, controlling the temperature by increasing and decreasing the input fuel under a controlled condition by technology of pneumatics, scanners and other complex devices for a safe operation. These units have been known to blow; when they did they could move three to four hundred tons of steel like it was a feather. These were big powerful furnaces that the steel industries use to melt down steel. The furnaces' applications in the citrus industry are the energy driver for the big cooker and drying orange peel into citrus pulp, making the mill a part of the pulp mill business. I am a tool maker, and I understood the operation. The only thing about all the trades I mentioned is, I got my welding certifications later when I got black balled,

## CHICKEN SCRATCH

during the time I fought the litigation of discrimination in the federal courts in Miami Florida.

Going back in time to the Virgil Mills moment at the mill and the role he played in this stage of my life. Virgil and I seem to be getting along good; he didn't interfere with the improvements nor did he tell me how to run the mill. He was learning from me. After all, I was the only person who knew more about the mill than anyone out there, and I had it producing. I modified shoot systems, lowered elevators, put in screw conveyors below the floor, and air operated dropout shoots. I explained to Mills what I was doing and the reason. I expressed to him the "why" and "cause" of what I needed to happen. Some of the things that I found out about later should have been done when the plant was built.

Well, one day I was told by Homer Caldwell, the maintenance supervisor, that they all were at the bar while Virgil was on vacation, and they were teasing him, telling him, "You might not have no job when you get back, because that nigger out there have damn near rebuilt the mill." When

Virgil returned to work, I didn't think anything about what I had done on the evaporator. I had installed a new oil system and added a drop out line to get the count on condensation. By timing, the water caught in the 55 gallon drum, and using a formula, would give the total evaporation capacity of the evaporator. This was very important because the operation was about evaporation. Therefore, the evaporation capacity needed to be known at all times, along with the energy used to drive off the moisture, and the amount of wasted energy due to tube installation from solids clinging to build up in the tube nest of 95½ inch tubes. This was the knowledge I knew in regards to the mill for some reason. I really had become a part of the system, or obsessed by it. Whatever it was, it had me drawn into it. Virgil began to treat me bad, like I was his enemy. He started doing things that would cause the operation to get off line. He would speed things up trying to make the dryer dry more than it could. I would not know he made these changes.

One day, my son Naz was sick. I asked Virgil for some time off so I could go with my wife to take Naz to the hospital because he was stiff. Virgil said, "You can't take off now." So

## CHICKEN SCRATCH

I gave my wife the insurance card, and she took off to the hospital. Naz remained there for ten days in intensive care. Mean time, Virgil got worse. He kept doing strange things. So I went to Wayne. My God—why did I do that? Virgil quit speaking. When he decided to speak to me, he told me that he appreciated that I went over his head and that I could take the job and shove it up my ass. Then, to shove it up Wayne's ass, and then we were to crawl up into Palmer's ass. I looked Mr. Mills directly into his eyes and said, "We both are men, and I hear everything you are saying. All I am going to say to you is, if you open your mouth and say one more foul word to me, referencing the mindset of a nigger, I am going to kick your ass right here. If you think that I am joking, try me." He stormed off, then Wayne came running out asking what happened. I told him nothing, and that Virgil was just having a bad day; everything was all right. At that point, I had gone as far as I could go and had taken all that I could take along this path. (Chicken scratch)

I knew then, that my knowledge of the mill had just saved my job, because you didn't talk that kind of trash in this neck of the woods to these people. Well, Virgil came out and he began to talk. We talked, and the both of us acted as if that had not taken place. As time moved ahead and my son Naz got better, I left and went to White Belt Ranch to work for Big John Dupre from Miami. This ranch was a 46,000 acre ranch.

This was a setback for me, because I took a job making $25.00 per day for seven days, and I grossed $150.00 a week. Yes, I made less. But I could not take that kind of treatment anymore. I had to go, even if it took me making less money for a while. Me having the carpenter trade, and Leo Machete, the foreman at White Belt Farms, needing two rooms built: 12'x24' additions—he hired me to do the renovation while I continued to work at White Belt Farms. This allowed me to earn a total of $525.00 a week.

In 1977, several months after I was gone, Virgil ripped the mill apart and demanded a big raise. Palmer Tuhill fired him and sent for me. This time, he made me superintendent over the mill, on a condition.

The condition was, if I could get the mill back together in 45 days, I would be put on salary along with all the other superintendents, on January 1, 1978. I met the deadline of getting the mill back together, and the plant started up on schedule. From that point on, it was an uphill battle with Wayne. Under no circumstances did Wayne Thomas want a black man in management, none whatsoever! Mr. Thomas was the production manager of the plant and the feed mill.

All the heads of departments worked under him. All the department heads managed one 8-hour shift. I was over three shifts and all the maintenance of the mill. The plant mill was a separate building from the feed mill. The date January 1, 1978 came, and with it, still no raise. In the months of February and March, there still was no change in my pay. I had done my part; the mill was operating better than it ever had. Each shift had operators that I trained one on one. My knowledge of the mill was reflected through these operators. The floors, the walls, were clean, and during the summer while I was rebuilding the mill, I also had seals built and installed on all the conveyors inside the mill, to prevent dust and other materials from escaping while operating. I developed a system of checking the mill continuously and each operator had learned this method.

The only problem me and other blacks had was, Wayne Thomas and those of authority that thought the way he did. I remembered what Paul had told me, that they did not want any niggers running no part of their operation. I heard Paul, but I knew better than that. They can't be that open with discrimination of this degree. Well, James Bush did it openly at Coca Cola with the book. I found out Paul was right, but I had to give them the benefit of the doubt. I did not want this to be the case where I found this new way of life, but I couldn't live it. I said, "*Oh* hell no, I am going to live that life. They are going to give me my money, just as they do all the others." (Chicken scratch)

The fight began with management. Wayne Thomas used every measure he could use against me. For five years on, and every day basically, I was discriminated against. He would not let up even when he would hire people to work in the mill. If they were white he would tell them, "I got an opening out there in the mill. I can give you a job if you don't mind working for a nigger." He would send drunks that he knew were drunks—people he knew would be harmful working in a place like the mill.

## CHICKEN SCRATCH

This man was something when it came to race. He would use blacks, putting blacks against each other, which was something he was very good at. It seemed like he took pure pleasure in it. There was a time he used a black man named Robert Willis against me in the mill. The mill was going so well, and I was on them about my money for the position as feed mill supervisor. They just were not going to let up at all. Wayne Thomas met Robert Willis and promised him that if he would come out to the feed mill and learn the operation, he would put him in charge and make him supervisor and put him on salary. It was the same thing they told me. When Robert asked him why, Wayne told him that they believed I was fucking with them, and with the mill. Because the place ran perfectly anytime I was around, but when I left the mill, something always went wrong. (Chicken Scratch)

What Mr. Thomas did not understand was that there were still problems with the system; the fact was that the mill was not complete, as to the equipment it needed. How does this make me feel now, as I look back with a terminal cancer? Oh, it is a feeling of feelings to reckon with the toils of life. Standing in a box of blades, flickering edges designed for cutting FLESH, waiting for one false move to create the fatal mistake. Standing there wondering, *why am I here?* God didn't have anything better to do, other than putting me in this box. How unfair would life be to me, a human being from childhood to old age?

Well, do you want to know something about it all? I really had no reason to give a damn? Maybe that is a problem I have from it all, is my humane building blocks became overwhelmed with understanding. Realizing racism and cancer bare the same side effects, they eat you alive, if not they put you into the box of blades. What I don't know is, how long I am going to be in remission, but what I do know is that I'm going to die. We all are. The idea of being told and suffering from the illness is the sign of factual evidence that the moment is coming. The breaking down of the human mind from racism is a real killer and will drive you below the radar of sanity. I almost had a nervous breakdown. I was put to sleep for a week from living under stress and fear for my family's safety. The hand of the most powerful, rich, and wealthy people released their bigots upon me to rip our lives apart, and they did just that. (Chicken Scratch) Understand, it's hard to read.

Terrie stuck with me. She stayed by my side even when it almost cost her LIFE. We went to hell and back as a family. Nazara, our son, was chased all the way to our front door, screaming at the top of his voice, because two strangers were trying to force him into their vehicle.

A young man called Captain Ike was murdered just down the road from our home. He was dragged, stabbed in the chest, acid poured in his face, and then hanged on the fence gate to the entry of the place where I repaired dumpsters. This crime is still unsolved. Terrie and I cooked on the street and sold barbecue to help bury the young man. We had the FBI investigate the area. I was placed under federal protection and was told to arm myself to defend my life if need be, to this very day.

I worked for these people, at this plant, for more than 10 years. That caused all this, and I took them to federal court and won.

# CHAPTER SEVEN

**WHEN I LOOK BACK AT** the games played upon me by the mind and heart of man, all I see is the vanity and trials of the times. From the window, viewing life, as it is now, causes me to wonder why life's rain feels so cold. "Yes, the vanity of vanities," says the preacher. Just look at how distorted my life was. No person should have to live like that, but there are many distorted lives out there. It's a real fire storm, (chicken scratch) in more than one way, to deal with the frame of mind. Knowing everything I have done for my family, the long-suffering by trial and illness, just to be told I am on cancer's death row, a sure termination. And there is nothing I can do but pray, wait, and hope for a cure in the medical world for others. I'm in remission, but I only have four months at this time as I write, according to man. I thank God it is not up to man. Even though we must rely on man and his technology of today, yet, it is better to have faith in God. (CHICKEN Scratch) Been into this for six years.

I started in 2008. I was 55 years old, not converted, nor filled with the Holy Ghost. Today, I am a minister of the gospel, and I believe I have a testimony of a lifetime. I am sitting here at the hospital with my wife, whom I've been married to for the past forty years. She had surgery back in 1986 on her esophagus, because the muscles became paralyzed and would not allow food to pass into her stomach. This type of procedure is known as a wrap. It's when the doctors lance the muscle of the esophagus where it separates from the stomach and turn it upward and wrap it around the esophagus, thus creating a narrow pathway for food to pass into the stomach. The problem with this picture was that the passageway closed off and would not allow food to go into her stomach. The tube filled up and she began to starve due to the food coming back up when she tried to eat. The tube was stretched open once before in 1989, and we were told that if the procedure was attempted again, to be warned, it might cause bleeding, and she might bleed to death. Now, here we are again. On May 2, 2013, a stent was put in and bleeding occurred. The stent remained in place for 32 days. It was removed June 5, 2013, at 9 am, a Wednesday.

Once the stent was removed, the bleeding stopped. Thursday, we underwent GI tests and an ultrasound on her leg and liver section. They could not find her gallbladder on this test. We were left wondering if her gallbladder had been removed from the previous surgery in 1986, and no one had informed us that it was removed, or if the ultrasound just couldn't find it. Well, today is Friday, June 7, 2013. She underwent a barium swallow test to see if all of it would pass into her stomach. It resulted that a large amount passed into her stomach, but some remained around the wrap. They saw some solids, but not much. The doctor will have to decide whether or not he will stretch the esophagus open more. That is a very high risk of a rupture, and if she starts bleeding, if that happens, God forbid, she will have to undergo major surgery to have her stomach reconstructed, and that's about a seven hour operation. (Chicken Scratch) Do you feel me?

## CHICKEN SCRATCH

You'd think this is all I had to deal with. Well, it's not—try problems of the family—my four sons. Not that I'm trying or wanting to be dad. Those days are long gone and have been for quite some time. I'm just their father. The only thing is, I took all my money and invested in all of them but Marculus, my youngest son. I am not talking a small amount. I'm talking about one million dollars. The rest went into my home and business, which was a welding company, certified by the department of transportation for the state of Florida, the state of Georgia, and the Solid Waste Authority of Palm Beach County, and Waste Management Inc. on a state level.

My oldest son, Tyrone Wendell Robinson, worked in the welding field; I set him up as Tyrone mobile welding. I set him up a shop on Savannah Avenue in downtown Valdosta. He found Jesus and left the business, and we can say he gave away the equipment I spent my money on, and funded his operation with for three years, at $80,000.00 a year, a total of $240,000.00 over the duration. Well, I didn't get that money back; instead I looked the other way, and yet kept my faith in my son that he was going to do the right thing.

It seems like, over the years, one day after twenty years of marriage, he and his wife just fell out of love.

So my wife and I ended up with all five of their children. When this comes up in discussion, my son will say, "I gave you my children so you guys could have a better income." That hurt, because he didn't really know the heavy load. The fact of just having a malignant terminal cancer was the weight of all weights. We really didn't need anything added to that. I went to Gainesville, Florida where my grandchildren had been abandoned, and when he heard we were there, he came home. When he met me, he said unto me, "Daddy, I have never been down so far in my life." I felt what he was saying deep down in my heart. He didn't know if I had the money, I would have given him as much as it would have taken to put his life back on track. I love my boys or young men. But the money was gone. It was his son Bud Jesus J. Robinson who came unto me and said, "Granddaddy, if things don't work out between my parents, and they somehow separate, will you take us in so that we don't become separated? Let us live with you and grandma please?" I was so moved that I responded with these words... "You all got a home as long as we live, and if anything goes wrong—we hope not—I promise you that you can come." That's how my grandchildren came into my life the way they did on my behalf.

On the other hand, my wife had spoken to my sons, without my knowing, asking them for their children so she could get some help. She told me later that she went to each one of them seeking help. Tyrone said, "Mom you can keep mine. Packman and my daughter Mikaela, please look after them for me, because Packman needs special attention and Mikaela is my only little girl. I want you to adopt three of them. But take care of all five."

Well, Tyrone's life is yet to get on track. He is working on it. He got his BS Degree in Psychology and is the owner of the Let's Eat Cafe. Please don't think I was putting him down; I'm just expressing the way that I see things from where I stand, at the corridor of life.

I really believe and think he is one of the best people I've ever known. He's also a minister of the gospel, and one day he will succeed, and things, through faith, will be alright. My next to the oldest son, Nazara Robinson, took over the welding business and he is doing GREAT. He is in a very good position to make millions of dollars. I don't understand him. I'm not getting into the issues, but they are very broad and complex. Overall, he is a very unique person, but has some real issues I can't really deal with. I will always be there for my son, regardless.

John C. Robinson, the architect, graduated from SCAD (Savannah College of Arts and Design) with his Masters. He also has issues that I really have to sit down to even talk about. But he also is a good person. When I think of his arena, I sweat, so I try not to go there. He has the capability to get things on the way. He doesn't do bad things, just doesn't do the right things (smile). Marculus, he seems to be on track. He is an engineer and very organized. He works for a very large engineering company. With his personality, skills, ability, and creative thinking, he should be able to excel in life. I want to get into details on each one of them, but it's best for me to leave it alone.

## CHICKEN SCRATCH

I just wanted to make a point about my life. I'm talking about me (Chicken Scratch) did you hear me?

In this same old place, I sit trying so hard to forget those suppressing moments in my life. But they just won't go away. I am forever scarred for life. It's by faith that I shall overcome. As I look and scan the trials dealing with cancer, the 42 radiation treatments killing the good cells and tissues along with the bad cells and tissues, over a period of time, the side effects deal with you in many different ways. I had burnt areas in my back, my chest, and both sides. The chemotherapy is the most devastating of all. It worked me over, killing all the immunity in my body. Inside my mouth, it seems like I had chewed up a mouth full of razor blades and swallowed them. These scars went down into my throat. This was very painful. I lost hair and all of my teeth except thirteen, and they are decaying from the results of the chemo. No doctor will remove them due to the fact of the mutation of bone cancer. Now, being that I've been in remission for a little over five years, they think it's safe for me to have them removed, and that's a good thing. (Chicken scratch) You heard me.

## JOHN ROBINSON

Out of everything I just describe about my family and what I face with the cancer, I'm yet to get over the stigma of discrimination and the role it plays in our lives. I'm now sixty years old and my mind is constantly scanning the memories for thoughts of the past and how life has really been to me. Aging is a new concept for me; I've never been old before. But I have been discriminated all the days of my life and now I witness it in the lives of others.

Even so, to console or condone is to conceal the traits of such a nasty disease, one that breaks you down from the heart. The evil, wicked, and ill-minded, being the true monsters of the human race. The venomous wills from their hearts, spewing out of their mouths, distorting, if not destroying, the lives of others in their common day. As if it's the way and the will of some god that they honor. In this will to be, a nation of power was formed, never to retreat, die first and kill the rest of the world in the process while they meet their death. This is the heartbeat of this mind that built a one world order, its region of power conquering the globe. (Chicken scratch)

## CHICKEN SCRATCH

It embodies, democracy being its tool, man's quest and thirst for freedom, with justice and liberty for all, by a set of amendments called the constitution as it reads: we the people, a political science used to govern and rule over its victims of oppression. Leaving them black classed; a people without a court or even a nation. I know because I am, and was a victim of its reckless behavior and lawyers, with a chaotic system of psychological mind-blowing discovery techniques just to sustain justice. I had the best of the best of lawyers; God had sent me a Moses Baker, Jack Scarola, Jeffrey Peterson, Peter Helwig and many more like Debbie Singer. They were a power pack in the courtroom. They fought a case under the Bush law, and you can only be discriminated against at the very moment of hire. (Chicken Scratch) Can you believe it?

The "very moment of hire" means, doing the interview for the job only after the review of the application, and you fill out the w-4 form. Once that was over, and you entered into the workplace, you could be called a Nigger, not given promotions, fired for any reason, and it was legal under the Bush Law of the land in 1989. I won, not because of the ramped discrimination, only because at the moment of hire, they put Mr. Rutledge on salary, and at my moment of hire, they put me on a time card and not salary. Now once we met that test, everything I charged them with could be brought in. Because of that law, 103 cases fell from the trial schedules to be heard, and these were major cases; only 3 cases of the original 105 remain standing, and my case was one of the three. We have to meet the test of the law, interpreted by legal scholars of the word of law or ministers of the law; being able to bring out the hidden agenda of the evil that's buried within the confines of the legal structure. Cases are not won by their merits, but how classically the merits are presented.

In the high courts the game change is about class, knowledge, money, and power. The client doesn't have to be the best of clients, just has to have a real case that can be tried by the courts. I was trapped by a thin hair-line thread called equal justice under the rules of law. Like I said, I went through the court system here in the United States of America. In fact, in Miami, Florida. Yes, the high courts of the United States Federal Court, the US District Judge, William

## CHICKEN SCRATCH

Hoeveler. As I fought this case, I was being transformed into another person driven by hardships. I refused to be broken by a system that casted it's net over me. Rendered helpless, I was emotionally drained of the hope I thought I had. A vein developed on the left and right sides of my forehead. They throbbed from every beat of my heart. I pissed solid blood for six months until I pass three gallstones. During those months, I slept on my hands and knees. I didn't have any insurance to see doctors; all I could do was pray and watch my family go through hell along with me. We went there (CHICKEN SCRATCH) please imagine the unseen lines.

Men that believe the black class of people, (note I didn't say race, I said class, by race), live a certain way because of the injustice in a free society. A people that are excluded from the mainstream of wealth of a nation, forced to live in the ghettos below poverty, and are labeled not capable of learning. My entire family, myself included, became the victims of such people. They robbed us of will and reason, leaving us standing there wondering, *why Lord is it still this way? How long must we endure?* They caused the joy to wither from our lives, like a flower in a hot summer without water.

## JOHN ROBINSON

The way it all started was, one day, Palmer Tuhill, the plant manager, and Wayne Thomas, the plant superintendent, decided to hire a man named Jack Rutledge to be the superintendent of the feed mill, to replace me. Mr. Rutledge had never been nor seen the inside of a mill before. They wanted me to train him for my position. They demoted me without cutting my pay on the hourly rate, kept me on the hour, placed him on salary. Salary at that time was around $50,000.00 to $70,000.00 a year, plus a vehicle and fuel to drive anyplace at any time, like your own personal truck or car, whichever you choose. As a result from their actions, I filed a complaint with the EEOC, the Equal Employment Opportunity Commission, in Miami, Florida. They found the company guilty on several accounts and issued me the notice of right to sue in the United States federal courts. (Chicken Scratch) Are we there yet?

Once I filed the complaint, I had to dig them a ditch, 14" wide, about 42" deep, for 250 yards, by hand, with round point and square point shovels. When I was almost finished digging the ditch, they started covering it back up, saying it was in the wrong location. The ditch never was dug again;

that was retaliation. They told me to quit, but they was not going to fire me. I got all the nasty jobs like removing old 55 gallon drums from around the plant scrap yard. These drums were maggot infested, and when I tried to remove them from the ground they would splash on me, one time in my face. I would not quit.

They assigned me to do very dangerous jobs, and more jobs than I could do in a day. They would write me up for failure of completion, but they wouldn't fire and I would not quit. Someone opened the main steam valve on the evaporator while I was performing maintenance on the unit. I barely escaped with my life, but I still would not quit. I was about eighty five feet in the air, on the top of this unit, inside a small area of handrail structure that was design for safety, to prevent a person from falling over the edge to their death. I was instructed by my now maintenance supervisor to check out the pop-off valve because they thought that it was sticking and not seating, thus releasing too much steam or energy. This big evaporator is only a cooker driven by blue steam produced by a 100,000 pound per cubic inch boiler. Which means 100,000 pounds of pressure are contained within a single cubic inch, produced by a big tube type boiler driven by natural gas as its energy source.

The pop-off valve's weight they had me check out was around 250 pounds or more, with a brace across the top that would only allow it to rise and fall about 10 or 12 inches if the pressure got too high in the unit, then it would release the excess steam into the atmosphere. In other words, the pop-off valve is a release valve. To work on this valve, you must be extremely careful. You have to make sure the boiler is on low fire and the king valve by-pass system is switched to the right circuit to prevent steam from entering the evaporator. The next step is to open all the steam valves on the bottom of the evaporator that let steam pressure off the unit. Well, I made sure all this was set up, along with the supervisor, before I went to the top of this big unit to look down into the pop-off valve, to examine it to see what could be causing it to stick as they claimed it was doing. (Chicken Scratch) Check out what's next

When I leaned over the top of the valve, I felt the unit shake. My God, it was steam coming up from the bottom of the unit. Just from the experience of being around these big units, I knew how to react: by leaning as far back as I could or as much as the handrail would allow me to move. I was confined in a small area, nowhere to move. I could only lean back. When the steam reached the pop-off valve, it raised the valve so violently that it broke the welds on the cross member that were designed to contain it. The noise it made was like a jet rowing in my ears. The sound was deafening, and all I could hear was ringing in my ears. An instant fear shattered all over me. My feet and hands felt like they were in a pillowcase of feathers. Someone just tried to kill me by turning the big boiler to hi-fire, closing off all the release valves on the bottom of the Evaporator, then opening king valve of the boiler, sending all this high pressure into the unit.

By the Grace of God, I escaped the harm that was headed my way. If by any chance the blue steam the color of cigarette smoke would have got me, I probably would have fallen or jumped from the top of the unit, 85 feet, to my DEATH. That was the kind of steam and pressure that was released on me. I most likely would have gone into a state of panic with my face and hair washed away from my skull from the blue steam blast. This was hell for me to write about (Oh Chicken Scratch) Life.

That's the type of stuff I went through out there. Then I would hear jokes like, "it's a crying shame that a bus loaded with niggers went over a deep cliff. That's just a shame. The crying shame would be if it had one empty seat." This was the general atmosphere around the place, over the edge. They fired me early one morning for refusing to pull some fence wire over live transformers. The only thing about this day was, my pay check was already made. I didn't have to wait on it like everyone else that got fired. They had decided that it was time for me to go. It was Homer's, the superintendent, day off and Denver McPeak was the acting foreman. He told me that he hated to ask me to keep on doing what Homer had me doing, which was moving the maggot infested drums from around the plant bone yard. He said I had the right to refuse doing a job that I knew was dangerous and that if they fired me because I refused to pull wire over the top of live transformers of 7200 volts, he would quit. They fired me, and I found out later that he did indeed quit.

## CHICKEN SCRATCH

Then, I got blackballed in six counties; Martin, Okeechobee, St. Lucie, Palm Beach, Broward, and Dade County. These good ole boys had a network and a shadow cast over me.

Now, allow me to tell you about what it's like, not what you think it's like, but what it is. As I fought the case in federal court, I started out alone with 17 witnesses that later became named plaintiffs, and that number became 44. Well, it was on. Now, I didn't have a job, couldn't get one, no company would hire me, and when they did, they would find out about the case and let me go. I still had a family to feed and take care of; that didn't change. The bank I did business with came to me and offered me a chance to work for myself by starting a business, a welding business. The president of the bank told me that I was about to go for a ride, for me to tie a knot in the rope and hold on, for I was about to take the ride of my life.

So they set me up not just for business, but for the kill when the time came, to break me down if I didn't comply with Caulkins demands to resolve the case. For starters, I had no job; the bank purchased me a three quarter ton pickup truck with a flatbed body for a brand new SA-200 Lincoln pipeline welder to set across the back. I was certified by the State of Florida Department of Transportation as a welder and became a certified minority business and did projects for the state for years. I worked for the major sanitation companies like the Solid Waste Authority, all county sanitation, and Waste Management.

There came the time when the case grew and was about to become a class action; that 44 number became 850 class members. Now, Caulkins wanted to settle the case with me and me alone, the attorney had me to come to Palm Beach to discuss the terms. They offered me $980,000.00 if I would settle alone without the class members. Without me, they had no case in the federal courts, but with me they did have a chance to be heard. Well, I refused to accept their offer. The statement to them was, my mother taught me to reserve myself for the last. Who am I to stand in the way of justice for so many people? When the word got back to them, they went to work on me. The bank no longer did business with me. They picked up everything we owned that was used for collateral. That was all the welding equipment and vehicles.

## CHICKEN SCRATCH

Now, we are stuck in a Jim Crow town with no means out. They paid blacks to harass me. Things began to get ugly. My joy began to melt down—even the church was afraid to get involved. They threw us out of their building one time when we were gathered as a class.

I found myself helpless for the very first time as a provider. To be broken down to a helpless stage by the hands and minds of those that hate you for whatever the reason... Is the state of stages to endure by faith for the absolute stability needed to survive? Endowed with hardships that I couldn't even began to believe were occurring in our lives as a family—to be turned inside out, driven into a maze of wonders, rambling and driven by rage to get through the maze and it seemed to be expanding the deeper I got into it.

I wanted to scream, but I knew it would be in vain, for no one around could hear me. Fixed in suffocation, trapped in the madness from the mind of furious men, hated for being black.

This madness began to seep from my heart into my mind causing me to become paranoid, panicking because I'm trapped. I felt that I was being driven, pushed over the edge. I got where I could not sleep for days. When I would fall to sleep, light would wake me. I had to have pitch black darkness without any sounds, if not, my eyes were open. We were getting threats like, "nigger get the hell out of town. How would you like it if dynamite is thrown into your home and kill your children?" I began to react in ways I never have acted in my life. Given my background, hell, I'm being squeezed to a point. I was slowly being driven into madness, to the point of welding a lawn mower's muffler to the barrel of a 22 magnum with a powerful expensive scope. I started carrying three pistols on me at all times: a 357 magnum, a 38 automatic, and a 45 caliber Smith and Wesson automatic. Plus, I hauled a M-1 in my truck everywhere I went, ready for battle anytime, Joe. Trapped by a thing called hate, and driven by pride. I'd rather have died at the battle than lose in the fight for justice. (Chicken scratch) Read the signs of madness.

I reached the place of darkness where no light appeared to shine. Compassion had withered from my heart and my mind no longer understood. I was a real bomb on the edge of exploding. Early one morning, I had made up my mind I was going to the plant and put an end to it all. (Chicken Scratch) look at what life has done to me.

Mr. Thomas and a few others were in serious trouble. It was their day to pay for all they had done to me. As I was preparing to go to the plant, my neighbor Jimmy Gary, Willie Gary's brother, asked me about my dogs. I snapped and I killed all my dogs, one with my son holding it in his hand, begging me not to kill his dog—almost killed my wife, stuck a hair trigger 25 automatic to a young lady's head because she would not wash the dishes like my wife asked her to. (Chicken Scratch) Look at the transformation of a man that was just a family person.

I was put to sleep for a week, put on a medication called Amitriptyline, an antidepressant. Then, I found myself to be lost within the maze surrounded by love. My wife and all my sons reached out and took me by the hand and they held me to let me know that I was still the love of their lives. They moved me toward God with that love. My lawyers were fighting like hell for me. To be discriminated takes a toll on your life in ways you would never believe, drive you to do thing's that's not a part of your character. I love my family with all my heart. The things I done was the part of me that was going to go to that plant and do something that would have taken me away from them for life. The feeling I had was empty. I felt like a nun fallen, by being a victim of rape.

Now, after all is said and done, will and reason, from the minds of the madness, I'm going to talk about the things we went through…There was times we didn't have food and I killed my neighbors hog and he told everyone in the neighborhood by yelling out loud, "this man done killed my biggest hog and got his children toting the meat out of the woods—just look at them." Well, I offered him a ham; other than that, it's best to leave the hog business alone. I was in a zone of live or die. It didn't matter. I was going to fight until the end. I became a certified welder by the company that did the Alaskan pipeline Trans Eastern, then later, with the department of transportation for the state of Florida and Georgia. I began to work on bridges and refurbishing sanitation equipment for companies like Waste Management and the Solid Waste Authority, on a large scale. (Chicken Scratch) Do you feel me?

Being able to work and earn a living on my own and nothing they could do to stop me because they made me become another person, and I'm glad about it. We are about to sign a contract with the city of Columbus, Georgia for over two million dollars; you see all things work for the good. I found out without choice that I had no choice but to deal with whatever they threw my way. I had a welding shop that I had leased, but I didn't move into immediately, because someone had left brand-new like ice cream equipment in the place. I was not about to throw their machinery out. I would not want that for myself if it were mine. Well, the people I leased the building from tried to get me to move in and test the units out. They asked, "When are you going to move the equipment?" I told them, "On a Thursday." Well, someone went by there and put pipe bombs in the units that we were going to move. The only problem was that they dropped one and it exploded, so the law came. They would not allow me to go to the site, and I had leased the building. Tobacco and Firearms came out and conducted the investigation. I was then placed under federal protection and was instructed to arm and defend myself. A few months later, in 1989 my family was attacked by Homer Caldwell's family, the maintenance superintendent from Caulkins—the company I had in court. Was it going to ever end well? In 1994 I finally won the case, some 12 years from the day I filed the first complaint with the EEOC in 1982.

Now as I look back with cancer and at the cancer of another kind, I say, which one is worse? Life must go on. I'm a positive thinker and our family is united—one bond, one LOVE. We will never yield nor stop because of a flawed system that overshadows America. Even though it seems like I've been to hell and back, yet I look to the hill, from which cometh my strength.

May God bless the reader of this book... (Chicken Scratch)

www.ingramcontent.com/pod-product-compliance
Lightning Source LLC
Chambersburg PA
CBHW070429010526
44118CB00014B/1970